# The Grand Review

## The Civil War Continues to Shape America

**Bold** Print, Inc.

York, Pennsylvania

Bold Print, Inc.
Published by Bold Print, Inc., 573 W. Market Street, York, PA 17404
First published in 2000 by Bold Print, Inc.

Printed in the United States of America

Designed by Bold Print, Inc.
www.grandreview.com

First edition

ISBN 0-9647123-2-6

# CONTENTS

# Acknowledgments

Many people have been involved in ensuring that this project turned from a dream into reality. We would like to thank those who helped. And to those not mentioned here, we thank you also.

Jonathan Webb. To our focus group members: James Beidler, Virgil Sova, Eleanor Boggs Shoemaker, Ruthe Fortenbaugh Craley, we thank you. Dr. Wayne Temple, who patiently answered questions on Mary Todd Lincoln; Jean Baker, who provided insight into Mrs. Lincoln; D. Brook Simpson, who provided insider information on Ulysses S. Grant; Scott Balthaser; Warren W. Wirebach; Edward Steers Jr.; Carolyn, Irvin and Margaret Kittrell. June Lloyd, Lila Fourhman and Donna Shermeyer of the York County Heritage Trust. Charles J. Elmore, who provided photographs; Troy Leib; Doris Sweeney, who provided much legwork; Kim Bauer of the Illinois State Historical Library, who told us about the unpublished letter written by Mrs. Lincoln; the Valentine Museum; the Library of Virginia; the library and photograph staff of the United States Army Military History Institute in Carlisle, Pennsylvania, and the Grand Review 2000 Committee.

# Illustration Credits

| FL | Frank Leslie's Illustrated Newspaper |
|---|---|
| HW | Harper's Weekly |
| ISHL | Illinois State Historical Library |
| LC | Library of Congress |
| LIA | Leib Image Archives |
| OHS | Ohio Historical Society |
| MOLLUS | Military Order of the Loyal Legion of the United States |
| USMHI | United States Army Military History Institute, Carlisle, Pa. |

The 1881 watercolor on the book cover, painted by James E. Taylor and entitled *The Grand Parade of General Sherman's Army in Washington*, was provided by the Ohio Historical Society.

"Historical judgment of war is subject to an inflexible law, either very imperfectly understood or very constantly lost sight of. Military writers love to fight over the campaigns of history exclusively by the rules of the professional chess-board, always subordinating, often totally ignoring the element of politics. This is a radical error. Every war is begun, dominated, and ended by political considerations; without a nation, without a Government, without money or credit, without popular enthusiasm which furnishes volunteers, or public support which endures conscription, there could be no army and no war — neither beginning nor end of methodical hostilities. War and politics, campaign and statecraft, are Siamese twins, inseparable and interdependent; and to talk of military operations without the direction and interference of an Administration is as absurd as to plan a campaign without recruits, pay, or rations."

John G. Nicolay and John Hay, Abraham Lincoln's biographers

"A popular Government, without popular information, or the means of acquiring it, is but a prologue to a farce or a tragedy; or perhaps, both. Knowledge will forever govern ignorance; and a people who mean to be their own governors must arm themselves with the power which knowledge gives."

James Madison, August 4, 1822

# Contributors

Georg R. Sheets is an author, historian and former director of the Simon Cameron Mansion Museum. He presents a well-researched story about a proud moment in the nation's history that is unfamiliar to many Americans. The emotions that built to a peak at the Grand Review make this an exciting tale of the power struggle between Cabinet officers and generals and the fierce rivalry among soldiers fighting for the same cause.

Dr. Charles Reagan Wilson is director of Southern Studies at the University of Mississippi at Oxford. He is co-editor of *The Encyclopedia of Southern Culture*, author of *Baptism in Blood: The Religion of the Lost Cause, 1868-1920* and *Judgment and Grace in Dixie: Southern Faiths from Faulkner to Elvis.* Dr. Wilson delivers an insightful look at the South from the Civil War to the 1970s. He points out religion's role in Southern culture and particularly how people in the South used religious ideals to cope with the loss of their struggle to secede.

Peter Applebome of the *New York Times* and author of *Dixie Rising: How the South is Shaping American Values, Politics and Culture* writes an essay that Americans must read. Mr. Applebome, who spent most of his adult life in the South, explains how there remains a regional divide in America and how some of the issues that led to the Civil War still exist today.

L. Douglas Wilder is a former governor of Virginia and the first African-American ever elected to that post. He is currently associated with Virginia Commonwealth University as Distinguished Professor at the Center for Public Policy as well as the Department of Political Science. In his essay, he points out that the country rallied to meet the challenge of the Year 2000 computer glitch, but he sees no similar unity or passion in our approach to many issues that divide Americans. Still, Mr. Wilder offers the country hope.

Dr. John F. Marszalek is a professor of history at Mississippi State University and a noted Civil War historian and author. He is the author of *Sherman: A Soldier's Passion for Order* and several other books of Civil War and African-American history. Dr. Marszalek is the editor of the Grand Review section of this book.

Bradley Schmehl is a nationally known Civil War artist. He provides original illustrations, some created just for this publication.

Part I

# The
# Grand Review

by Georg R. Sheets

An original ticket for the Grand Review.

Edited by John F. Marszalek

LIA

**Edwin McMasters Stanton:** Born Dec. 19, 1814, in Ohio. Died Dec. 24, 1869, in Washington, D.C. An attorney, he left a law practice to become the U.S. Attorney General in 1860. He became President Lincoln's second War Secretary in 1862. In December of 1869, President Grant appointed him to the Supreme Court. He died before he could be sworn in. His picture was on the $1 bill around 1890.

**Jefferson F. Davis:** Born June 3, 1808, in Kentucky. Died Dec. 6, 1889, in New Orleans. An 1828 graduate of West Point. A Mississippi planter, he served in the Mexican War. He served as War Secretary under President Pierce and resigned from the U.S. Senate when Mississippi seceded. On Feb. 18, 1861, he was inaugurated as the President of the Confederacy. In 1866, he was indicted on charges of treason. The case was dropped.

**Mary Todd Lincoln:** Born Dec. 13, 1818, in Kentucky. Died July 16, 1882, in Illinois. The daughter of a prominent family, she married Abraham Lincoln on Nov. 4, 1842. During the White House years she was called "Madam President." She spiraled into depression after the death of her son Willie, the assassination of her husband and the death of her youngest son, Tad, in 1871. Son Robert had her committed as insane in 1871. A judge ruled she was sane less than a year later.

LIA

**Abraham Lincoln:** Born Feb. 12, 1809, in Kentucky. Died April 15, 1865, in Washington, D.C. The 16th President. He served in the Illinois Legislature and was licensed to practice law. Elected to the House of Representatives, where he opposed the Mexican War. He became a presidential candidate in the Republican Party and won the 1860 election. The writer of the Emancipation Proclamation and the Gettysburg Address, Lincoln was re-elected in 1864. He became the first president to be assassinated.

LIA

**Ulysses S. Grant:** Born April 27, 1822, in Ohio. Died July 23, 1885, in New York. Christened Hiram Ulysses Grant. The 18th President. Graduated from West Point in 1843, 21st in a class of 39. Served in the Mexican War. Before the Civil War, he failed at farming and real estate and worked in his father's leather shop. He received the nickname "Unconditional Surrender." One of the first three Americans to receive the rank of lieutenant general. Elected President on the Republican ticket in 1869 and was re-elected. Lost his fortune but recouped some of it for his family by writing his memoirs.

**Robert E. Lee:** Born Jan. 19, 1807, in Virginia. Died Oct. 12, 1870, in Virginia. Graduated from West Point in 1829. Married the great-granddaughter of Martha Washington. Served in the Mexican War and was superintendent of West Point. He commanded the troops that put down John Brown's raid at Harper's Ferry. He declined President Lincoln's offer of Union field commander and chose to be loyal to Virginia during the Civil War. After the war, he was president of Washington College, later renamed Washington and Lee University.

**Joseph Eggleston Johnston:** Born Feb. 3, 1807, in Virginia. Died March 21, 1891, in Washington, D.C. Graduated from West Point in 1829. Served in the Mexican War, where he was wounded. After the secession, he left the U.S. Army and joined the Confederate Army, where he was commissioned as brigadier general. After the war, he was an honorary pallbearer at William T. Sherman's funeral, where he refused to put on his hat in the brisk wind. He died five weeks later.

LIA

**William Tecumseh Sherman:** Born Feb. 8, 1820, in Ohio. Died Feb. 14, 1891, in New York. Graduated from West Point in 1840. Served in the Mexican War. He married the daughter of his foster parents. Resigned from the Army to become the local agent in San Francisco for a St. Louis-based bank. When the bank failed, he practiced law briefly in Kansas and then served as superintendent of Louisiana Military Seminary. In 1869, he became commander of the Army until his retirement in 1883.

LIA

*The Compromises of the 1850s only delayed the inevitable.*
*Brick by brick, a wall was erected between the North and the South that*
*impaired a clear vision of the country's future. Blocking the line of sight were the*
*question of slavery, the rights of states and a towering difference in cultures. Emotions flared.*
*Men's hearts hardened. In 1861, they decreed that the only way to settle their differences was by*
*CIVIL WAR.*

Under the darkening skies of April 9, 1865, telegraph lines crackled with the message that would change the world: Lee had surrendered to Grant at Appomattox. A few weeks later, the news came of Johnston's surrender to Sherman in North Carolina. The South was lost. Victory and power to the Union!

After four years of civil war, America finally sighed and then realized its worst nightmare. Confederate and Union soldiers had fought in nearly 10,000 battles, from skirmishes to epic struggles that left more than 620,000 soldiers dead, more than 500,000 wounded. The war's direct costs exceeded $5 billion. But these figures were almost meaningless as people took account of the war's devastating effects on their families, their towns and their states.[1]

In the North, a celebration acknowledging the end of the war was in order.

On May 18, 1865, the army issued Special Orders No. 239, calling for a Grand Review, a two-day parade in Washington, D.C., of the main Union armies. On May 23, the Army of the Potomac would march down Pennsylvania Avenue. Soldiers of the armies of Georgia and the Tennessee would take center stage the next day. In all, more than 150,000 soldiers would parade through the nation's capital, filing past the President and his cabinet as well as Lt. Gen. Ulysses S. Grant positioned on a special reviewing stand in front of the White House.

The country had never witnessed a military and civilian display so large and so charged with emotion. As word spread, spectators, numbering hundreds of thousands, poured into the city and occupied curbs, windows and balconies for a mile and a half from the Capitol to the White House. They came to see the soldiers and politicians they had read of in news dispatches. These were America's heroes. Not since the Revolutionary War had ordinary people — some failures as civilians, many hungry for power — ascended to such prominence.

The Grand Review evolved into something larger than an historic event to mark the end of the Civil War. It showcased America's military strength to the world, providing proof to leaders on every continent that America could raise armies and bring her people to the defense of their Constitution.

A federal holiday in Washington was declared for the two-day parade. The government shut down; schools closed. The sale of alcohol was prohibited. The judge in the assassination trial of President Abraham Lincoln postponed testimony. And on a sad note, the grieving and resentful wife of the first assassinated U.S. President left the White House with her two sons almost unnoticed during the fanfare.

For some of the soldiers, marching in the Grand Review was just one more military order to fulfill; to others, it was closure to four years of war. To the public, it exposed the East-versus-West rivalry that existed between the Union armies.

The days before the Grand Review found the nation's capital tense. Lincoln's assassination had left government officials nervous and uncertain. Politicians jockeyed for power. Reconstruction of the South demanded attention. And one great but bitter general arrived with his loyal army determined to regain his honor — "COST WHAT IT MIGHT."

# Politics of War

## Silence Your Opponents

## 'No Law Here Except Mine'

The tension that would engulf the Grand Review surfaced in January 1865. A sickly Secretary of War Edwin McMasters Stanton decided to make an unannounced visit to William T. Sherman during one of the proudest moments in the major general's military career. Sherman had just captured Savannah, Georgia, in late December and offered the city as a gift to President Lincoln.

Headlines proclaimed Sherman's gesture, and a magazine cartoon depicted him as Santa Claus. Congress passed a resolution of praise. Letters from all over the nation lauded the conquering hero.[2]

Sherman was basking in the spotlight. He told his "sworn friend," Lt. Gen. Grant, he believed his army had "a confidence in itself that makes it almost invincible." [3]

The more chaos and destruction Sherman and his army had caused, the more popular he had become in the North. And now his old nemesis, the press, loved him. Sherman distrusted the press and regarded reporters as spies. In 1863, he ordered the arrest and court-marital of a reporter.[4]

After failing as a California banker in the 1850s and being labeled "insane" in Kentucky in 1861, Sherman was at last experiencing the success he desired.[5] He had vowed to make "Georgia howl," and his devastating march from Atlanta to Savannah in 1864 made good on

*USMHI/FL*

SANTA CLAUS SHERMAN PUTTING SAVANNAH INTO UNCLE SAM'S STOCKING.

this promise. He cut Confederate railroad, communication and supply lines. He demoralized rebel soldiers by showing them they could not fight the Union and, at the same time, protect their women and children from his army.[6]

Sherman did not hate Southerners, but most of them feared him because of the destruction wreaked by his army. Sherman was a soldier and viewed the 11 Southern states that seceded from the Union as Americans who had lost their way. [7]

Sherman telegraphed President Lincoln on December 22, 1864, with the news of Savannah's fall.

"I beg to present you as a Christmas present the city of Savannah, with one hundred and fifty heavy guns and plenty of ammunition, also about twenty-five thousands bales of cotton." Lincoln wrote Sherman on December 26 expressing "Many, many thanks. ..." [8]

Not everyone stood in line waiting to praise Cump, as Sherman was called by his family. Sherman's popularity worried Secretary of War Stanton and the radicals of the Republican Party. They shuddered when the Democratic Party considered him as a possible presidential choice and the *New York Herald* called on Lincoln to step down so the Republican Party could unite on a Grant and Sherman presidential ticket in 1864.[9] Sherman was not a politician and had said he would prefer the penitentiary to the presidency.[10]

*USMHI*
The Emancipation Proclamation signing.

Sherman also became an embarrassment to Lincoln when he refused to obey the President's Emancipation Proclamation, a war document that freed slaves only in rebellious states on January 1, 1863, and allowed their enlistment into the Union military.[11] When news of Sherman's opposition to Lincoln was published, abolitionists reviled him while Southerners praised him.[12] Lincoln, who had wrestled with the question of arming blacks since taking office, telegraphed Sherman, asking the general to obey the law.[13] Sherman still refused and showed his contempt when the government shipped a black infantry regiment to his command after Savannah's fall. Before these soldiers could show their military grit, the black regiment was stripped of its arms and reduced to laborers, teamsters and servants. Sherman believed black men would not fight. Some of Sherman's men harassed the new regiment, killing a couple of the trained fighters and wounding others. These Union soldiers had taken on the anti-black sentiments of their commander.[14]

Sherman's position also was contrary to that of Stanton, who wanted to arm slaves, and the Radical Republicans, who wanted the slaves freed and equipped with the right to vote.[15] The Secretary of War believed the slave was "the main prop" holding up the Confederates' ability to wage war, and he silently supported field commanders who freed and armed slaves in their territories before Lincoln supported the move.[16]

Working behind the scenes in the Confederate army, slaves and paid Southern free blacks helped to build and to maintain the infrastructure that allowed the rebel government to wage war. Nearly invisible, they worked as laborers, machinists, carpenters, blacksmiths, masons, farmhands cooks, and boat makers. The Confederate government enacted laws permitting payment to slave owners for their workers and levied fines on slave masters who did not provide black labor to the Confederate cause. Eventually, in a state of desperation, Confederate President Jefferson Davis attempted to turn slave labor into military power. On March 13, 1865, he signed a bill allowing the enlistment of slaves in the rebel army. But the bill came too late.[17]

*LC*
Black workers laboring on the docks.

©*Bradley Schmehl*

The Sherman-Stanton rift would come to an historic climax on the second day of the
Grand Review.

"From the moment Mr. Stanton became Secretary of War, he never relaxed his efforts to destroy slavery in the rebellious territory as the surest and cheapest, if not the only, salvation of the Union, and to win Mr. Lincoln over to that way of thinking," Union Gen. E.D. Townsend said.[18]

The arming of slaves was such a delicate topic in 1861 that it caused Lincoln to basically fire Stanton's predecessor, Simon Cameron, the troublesome Pennsylvania politician. Lincoln had been looking for a way to rid himself of Cameron, his first Secretary of War, because of the Pennsylvanian's past transgressions and his inability to operate an efficient department. The last straw for Lincoln occurred when Cameron decided to include a paragraph on arming blacks in his report to Congress.[19] Lincoln demanded that Cameron remove the paragraph, but the Secretary of War had already sent copies to newspapers. Lincoln removed the paragraph. This resulted in the public and Congress receiving different versions of Cameron's report.[20]

*USMHI*

Simon Cameron

The great irony was Cameron did not write the paragraph that incensed Lincoln — Stanton wrote it. Cameron had sought legal advice of Stanton. Knowingly or unknowingly, Stanton prepared the way for Cameron's downfall. In January 1862, Lincoln sent Cameron to Russia as ambassador and appointed Stanton as his second Secretary of War.[21]

The subject of freeing and arming slaves was hotly debated across the country. Abolitionists, such as Frederick Douglass and William Lloyd Garrison; soldiers, such as Maj. Gen. David Hunter; journalists, such as Horace Greeley, politicians and others leaned on Lincoln to make a decision. Congress pushed Lincoln to emancipation when members passed on July 17, 1862, the second Confiscation Act and the Militia Act.[22] Section II of the Confiscation Act, instigated by Stanton, freed slaves whose owners aided the Confederacy and authorized the President to organize black troops. A section of the Militia Act provided a salary for these troops, which was prohibited by army regulations of 1816. Lincoln wanted to veto the Confiscation Act because he believed only the President held the power to free the slaves. Lincoln agreed to sign the bill, but he took the unprecedented step of placing before Congress his statement of objections.[23]

The Confederates did not sit idly as Lincoln freed the slaves. The Confederate Congress passed a law in May 1863 that any Union commissioned officers in command of African troops, when captured, be put to death for "inciting servile insurrections," and that any black Union soldier taken prisoner be sold into slavery or executed. Rebel soldiers on more than one occasion followed the law and killed captured black Union soldiers and officers.[24]

Before the 1864 presidential election, a contest Lincoln believed he would lose, Lincoln pointed out the flaws in the

*LC*

Black soldiers on garrison duty.

Democratic Party platform. The Peace Democrats were calling the war a failure and wanted it stopped immediately. Lincoln said the Peace Democrats wanted to return to slavery the 200,000 blacks in the Union army. [25]

"We shall have to fight two nations instead of one," the President explained. The Union cause would be bleak if "you fling the compulsory labor of millions of black men into (the Confederate) side of the scale. Abandon all the posts now garrisoned by black men; put them in the battle-field or cornfield against us, and we would be compelled to abandon the war in three weeks." [26]

In May 1863, Stanton established a separate bureau in the War Department to handle black volunteers. He also sent Adjutant-General Lorenzo Thomas through the South to promote black enlistment and to discipline officers who opposed the policy.[27] Thomas complained to Stanton that the biggest opponent of this policy was Cump Sherman, the most popular soldier in the North next to Grant.[28]

While en route to Savannah in January 1865, Stanton wrote Grant advising him to urge Sherman to organize black troops. "He does not seem to appreciate the importance of this measure and appears indifferent if not hostile," Stanton wrote.[29]

Sherman was far from Washington, waging war, and he did not agree with the government's position on the arming of blacks. He had to be taught a lesson, and "The Mad Incorruptible," as Stanton was called, was to be his private tutor.[30]

Stanton, too, had experienced celebrity status. In 1859, he was one of the attorneys on Congressman Daniel Sickles' defense team. The lawyers argued that Sickles had fatally shot his wife's lover, Philip Barton Key — son of the composer of the "Star Spangled Banner" — on February 27, 1859, due to temporary insanity. This was one of the first uses of such a plea. Sickles walked away a free man and returned to his wife.[31]

After Lincoln appointed him Secretary of War, Stanton became one of the most powerful men in America.[32] He demanded respect and in many cases inspired fear.[33]

LIA

Daniel Sickles

Stanton, the only Democrat in Lincoln's cabinet, who had been critical of Lincoln before joining his staff, was a bull dog who "cared nothing for the feelings of others" and "felt no hesitation in assuming the functions of the president or in acting without advising with him," Grant said in his memoirs.[34]

Soon after taking office, Stanton seized the new technology of telegraph communications and placed transmitters and receivers in rooms next to his office.[35] This led Lincoln to develop the habit of taking frequent trips from the White House to the War Department where he could learn the military activities of the day.[36]

The Civil War was big business and many stood in line to profit from it. Stanton stopped corrupt businessmen from defrauding the government. [37]

He upset foreign leaders as well as some businessmen and American politicians when he revoked all foreign contracts for military items that could be produced in the United States. "Made in America" created a boom for U.S. businesses and helped lift American factories from depression. But in many quarters, Stanton's edicts made him a hated man, and some people wanted him removed from office. [38]

"If you will find another Secretary of War like him," Lincoln would tell any foe of Stanton's, "I will gladly appoint him."

Stanton ran the War Department with a heavy hand, but it was Lincoln who had dominion over

Maj. Gen. Henry W. Halleck

his cabinet and the government. Nevertheless, Lincoln appreciated the unyielding strength of the Secretary of War he called "Mars." [39]

"He is the rock on the beach of our national ocean against which the breakers dash and roar ... without ceasing," Lincoln said of Stanton. "He fights back the angry waters and prevents them from undermining and overwhelming the land. Gentleman, I do not see how he survives, why he is not crushed and torn to pieces. Without him I should be destroyed." [40]

Before Stanton left Washington for Savannah, Union Maj. Gen. Henry W. Halleck wrote to Sherman, his friend since 1846, and cautioned Cump that his popularity magnified his pro-slavery views. "Old Brains," as Halleck was called, warned that officials close to the President planned to make an example of Sherman because he had an "almost criminal dislike to the negro, and that you are not willing to carry out the wishes of the Government in regard to him, but repulse him with contempt."

Writing from Washington, Halleck told his friend that the "leading men in the administration" believed Sherman could have brought 50,000 freedmen to Savannah from Atlanta during "your great raid," thus stripping Georgia of laborers and opening an escape route for slaves. Instead, the leaders pointed out, Sherman had cut the bridges and "caused the massacre of large numbers by Wheeler's cavalry."

Halleck then suggested that Sherman reopen any escape routes for slaves and consider allowing the freedmen to occupy "the rice and cotton plantations on the coast." Halleck told Sherman that bringing the slaves "within our lines will do much to silence your opponents. You will appreciate my motives in writing this private letter." [41]

Friends also cautioned Sherman that his position was out of line with the government. A couple of days after receiving Halleck's warning, Sherman read a January 2, 1865, letter from recently appointed Supreme Court Chief Justice Salmon P. Chase concerning the "apparent harshness of your actions towards the blacks." This Republican leader, a supporter of Sherman, told Cump, "You are understood to be opposed to their employment as soldiers and to regard them as a set of pariahs, almost without rights." Chase told Sherman to set an example for his troops. [42]

Freed slaves follow Sherman's army in great numbers.
Some would participate in the Grand Review.

Sherman's views did not concern many Georgia blacks. They had been praying for a "Moses" to free them from their "pharaoh," and when William Tecumseh Sherman arrived, many believed he was their savior. About 15,000 freed slaves had "shaken off the shackles forever" and arrived in Savannah from Atlanta with his army, the *New York Herald* reported.[43]

"They gather round me in crowds, and I can't find out whether I am Moses or Aaron, or which of the prophets; but surely I am rated as one of the congregation," Sherman told Halleck.[44]

Still weakened from the stresses of Lincoln's 1864 re-election campaign, Stanton, along with other politicians and visitors, finally stepped ashore in Savannah on January 11, 1865. After some formalities — Sherman showed them the condition of his troops and talked to Stanton about the confiscated cotton — the War Secretary discussed with Sherman the "negro question." Stanton told Sherman to arrange a meeting with local blacks for Stanton to interview.[45]

This insulted Sherman, but it was consistent with Stanton's goals.[46] Two months after the Emancipation Proclamation became law, Stanton's Freedmen's Inquiry Commission was charged to investigate and to report on "how (blacks) can be most usefully employed in the service of the Government for the suppression of the Rebellion."[47]

Now, Stanton was in Savannah to personally conduct the commission's work. He would confront the loudest and most popular opponent of this policy — Sherman.

Unknown to Sherman, he was about to be put on trial for his transgressions.

Sherman and Stanton were like vinegar and oil. Sherman was just over 6 feet tall and lean, with reddish-brown hair, piercing black eyes and a face lined with wrinkles. He was a nervous man, prone to excessive talking laced with profanity. He was lively and quick to devise an idea — often without reflection.[48]

Stanton, on the other hand, was a short, thick, dark man with a very large head and a mass of black hair. He was intense, religious and entirely absorbed in his duty, earning him the nickname "The Great Energy." Stanton found it difficult to strike agreements with men of Sherman's temperament.[49]

But Stanton could be just as impulsive and quick to act as Sherman. A couple of months after he became Secretary of War, Stanton worried about the South's ownership of the battleship Merrimac. He came to the conclusion that the ship could cause problems to major cities on the East Coast, including Washington. He devised a plan to stop the Merrimac's path to the nation's capital. Stanton wanted to load canal boats with rocks and sink them in the Potomac River.

Secretary of the Navy Gideon Welles thought Stanton's plan was silly and expressed his thoughts to Lincoln. The President listened with interest to Stanton's reasoning, but finally sided with Welles, a man with a full white beard whom he called "Neptune."

While Lincoln, with Stanton, Welles and others, was traveling down the Potomac on a steamer, someone inquired about the 60 or more canal boats on the shore.

"Oh," the President said, "that's Stanton's navy. That is the fleet concerning which he and Mr. Welles became so excited in my room. Welles was incensed and opposed the scheme, and it has proven that Neptune was right. Stanton's navy is as useless as the paps (nipples) of a man to a sucking child. There may be some show to amuse the child, but they are good for nothing for service."[50]

*LC*

Jefferson C. Davis

In Savannah, Stanton set the tone for his visit by showing Sherman a *New York Tribune* article about the December 9, 1864, incident at Ebenezer Creek.[51]

Between Augusta and Savannah, Sherman's 14th Corps commander, Jefferson C. Davis (not Confederate President Jefferson F. Davis), had ordered a portable bridge moved after his troops used it to cross the swollen creek. Hundreds of blacks, mainly women, children and older men, had rushed forward to use the same bridge, but they were too late. Joseph Wheeler's Confederate cavalry was approaching from behind, and the freed slaves panicked. Some jumped into the water and drowned. Others swam safely to shore. Those left on the opposite shore met unknown fates. Some reports said they were butchered; others said they were taken back into captivity.[52]

*LIA*

Joseph Wheeler

Davis' action incensed some of his soldiers. One officer called the incident "inhuman, barbarous" and wrote to his congressman. Eventually, the contents of the letter ended up in the *New York Tribune* story and on the desk of Secretary of War Stanton.[53] Davis, a pro-slavery Democrat who out of earshot was sometimes called "General Reb," was summoned. When questioned, he explained to Stanton and Sherman that he needed the pontoon bridge immediately. He believed Wheeler's men did not kill any of the blacks. Sherman called the incident a "cock and bull" story and stood by Davis, who never mentioned it in his monthly report.[54]

On January 12, 1865, Stanton interviewed 20 black men — 15 of whom were former slaves — selected by Sherman. Nearly all were ministers or church laymen. One man, Jacob Godfrey, told Stanton he was in the rebel army. At 8 p.m., Stanton began the interview in a room Sherman rented at the Green House. The men chose the Rev. Garrison Fraizer as their spokesman.[55]

Fraizer delivered thoughtful answers to Stanton's questions. Stanton wanted to know if blacks understood Lincoln's emancipation order — Fraizer said they did — and if blacks desired segregation, to which 19 answered yes. Stanton also asked if blacks would serve in the rebel army. Only by force, Fraizer said.

Sherman listened quietly as Stanton's assistant wrote down eleven of the answers. What happened next left Cump Sherman angry. The Secretary of War told Sherman to leave the room because the 12th question was about him. Stanton waited, then asked Fraizer, "State what is the feeling of the colored people toward General Sherman, and how far do they regard his sentiments and

Rev. Ulysses L. Houston

Alexander Harris

Rev. William J. Campbell

These are three of the men who were present at the Green House during Stanton's interview.

*Charles J. Elmore*

8

actions as friendly to their right and interest or otherwise."

Fraizer answered, "We look upon General Sherman, prior to his arrival, as a man, in the providence of God, specially set apart to accomplish this work. ... We have confidence in General Sherman."

Long after the emotions of the hour had cooled, Sherman observed, "It certainly was a strange fact that the great War Secretary should have catechized negroes concerning the character of a general who had commanded a hundred thousand men successfully across four hundred miles of hostile territory, and had just brought tens of thousands of freedmen to a place of security; but because I had not loaded down my army by other hundreds of thousands of poor negroes, I was construed by others as hostile to the black race." [56]

After the meeting, Stanton sought constructive action. According to Gen. Rufus Saxton, who accompanied Stanton to Savannah as the commander of the freedmen, abandoned lands and the organization of colored troops in the Department of the South, Sherman told Stanton to "leave the question of the freedmen in the territory conquered by my army to me. I have it all fixed up." Stanton turned to Saxton and with a hint of sarcasm said, "General Sherman wants to have charge of the freedmen's interest. We must leave it to him." [57]

What resulted was a revolutionary land-reform and race-relation document, Special Field Orders No. 15, written by Sherman with Stanton's editorial assistance. The order, released four days later, represented a total reversal of Sherman's pro-slavery stance. It included sections on the enlistment of black soldiers and promised each freedman 40 acres of land on prime property confiscated by the federal government. Republican Sen. Thaddeus Stevens of Pennsylvania later interpreted the document to read "forty acres and a mule" as he debated its importance before Congress.[58]

The Secretary of War worried that the orders might be "contrary to law." Saxton said Sherman responded, "There is no law here except mine, Mr. Secretary." Stanton opposed parts of the order but did not fight it, said Saxton, who was placed in charge of the program.[59]

Ellen Sherman

Returning to Washington, Stanton telegraphed Grant on January 17, 1865, with a message about his dealings with Sherman. "I staid [sic] with Sherman four days and would be glad to see you so as to communicate some other matters that cannot be safely written." [60]

The day Stanton left Savannah, January 15, 1865, Sherman wrote to his wife, Ellen. "Mr. Stanton has been here and is cured of that Negro nonsense." [61]

Sherman wrote to Halleck, thanking him for the warning. Sherman witnessed the attempt to use him as an example concerning the Negro question, and the Rev. Fraizer may have spared him.

"There is no doubt that Mr. Stanton, when he reached Savannah, shared these thoughts," Sherman said, "but luckily the negroes themselves convinced him that he was in error, and that they understood their own interests far better than did the men in Washington, who tried to make political capital out of this negro question." [62]

Sherman did not stay in Savannah long enough to see how his order was carried out. (The land given to 40,000 freedmen was returned to white Southerners in August 1865, nearly two months after the former slaves took it over.[63])

In Washington, Stanton gave the cabinet a vague report on his trip to Savannah, saying he went there for rest. Secretary of the Navy Welles suspected Stanton went there to "pay court" to Sherman and become his friend.[64]

# Forage Liberally

## Bummers Invade the South

## 'We'll See About This Peace Business'

Stanton's visit left some of Sherman's soldiers upset. One called the War Secretary "boorish" and hailed his departure. The soldiers did not appreciate anyone meddling with the general they called "Uncle Billy." Sherman's soldiers would address Stanton's demeanor in Savannah at the Grand Review.[1]

Sherman had forged a strong relationship with his soldiers. Before leaving Atlanta in 1864, he thinned the ranks, keeping mostly veterans. Many were Western soldiers, the sons and grandsons of pioneers, who learned the art of battle fighting Native American warriors. While marching through the South, some expressed outrage over this war. Dealing with the institution of slavery, some believed, was not worth the lives of comrades and family members.[2]

Sherman told a group of Southern businessmen before his soldiers set fire to their mills, "Gentlemen, niggers and cotton caused this war, and I wish they were both in Hell." [3]

Some of Sherman's soldiers were able to vent their anger on black and white Southerners after Uncle Billy issued orders to "forage liberally." Once Grant approved Sherman's march from Atlanta to Savannah, Sherman cut his own communication and supply lines. His soldiers had to live off the land and its people. This was not the first army to feed itself by foraging, but Sherman's men turned the practice into an art. Sherman told his wife his soldiers took to foraging like "ducks to water." [4]

The core group of foragers became known as the "bummers." They despised army routine and wanted excitement, willingly accepting great risks to get it. These rough-looking soldiers intimidated with a look, a word or just a tilt of the head. They preferred ragged, ill-fitting clothes. They slouched, crawled and climbed trees in the Native American style. Some were barefoot, and some cursed and spit tobacco just to see the effect on Southern aristocrats. But all the foragers had a skill in finding food to feed Sherman's army.[5]

They would start in the morning on foot, returning in the evening mounted on horses or mules loaded with food and sometimes valuables.[6] Bummers and

*USMHI*

A bummer rides off with his booty.

other foragers would arrive in waves at Southern houses. What the first set of foragers missed the bummers would surely find.[7]

"In a few minutes our house was filled with the surging mass," a Southern woman remembered of the time Sherman's army marched through Sandersville, Georgia. "In a little while there was not a piece of china, silver or even the table cloth left, and the food disappeared in a second. Fences were torn down, hogs shot, cows butchered, women crying, children screaming, pandemonium reigned." [8]

Always in advance of the army, Sherman's bummers seized key towns and railroads and reported Confederate movements.[9]

Bummers were so well-known that Southerners would hide their food and valuables.[10] So the bummers enlisted blacks to help search plantations, looking for freshly turned earth, searching swamps for hidden cattle, horses and other animals. The cabins of slaves were searched. Few hiding places fooled the bummers' instincts and pioneer skills.[11]

If the bummers arrived at a plantation and the owner declared there was no food, the bummers might enlist the help of a slave under the threat of death. If a slave was deemed honest, the bummers would let him go. Then the bummers might threaten to torch the plantation, forcing the hand of the owner.[12]

Bummers were a menacing group. But on a few occasions, the Union foragers actually helped Southern women hide their goods in exchange for all the food they could cart off. It was a vicious cycle, and stuck in the middle were the women and children whose husbands and fathers were off at war.[13]

As Sherman's soldiers marched to the sea, the two wings of this 60,000-strong army had cut a path of destruction through the South that left a lasting impression on its inhabitants.

When Sherman's army reached a Southern town, soldiers would camp anywhere they wished. They took control of houses and occupants. When they broke camp, the soldiers would leave a mess offending the senses.

"The fields were trampled down and the road was lined with carcasses of horses, hogs and cattle that the invaders, unable either to consume or to carry away with them, had wantonly shot down to starve out the people and prevent them from making their crops," a Southern woman wrote in her diary. "The stench in some places was unbearable; every few hundred yards we had to hold our noses or stop them with the Cologne." [14]

When Sherman's army was not eating, pillaging, marching or burning cotton mills, arsenals and homes, it

*USMHI/FL*

Sherman's bummers at work.

was cutting Confederate communication lines and destroying railroad tracks, sometimes by bending the heated steel around trees into what the soldiers called a "Sherman Necktie."

"The R.R. (railroad) track was torn up and the iron twisted into every conceivable shape," another Southern woman wrote in her diary. "Some of it was wrapped round the trunks of trees, as if the cruel invaders ... must spend their malice on the innocent trees of the forest, whose only fault was that they grew on Southern soil." [15]

Confederate soldiers had little patience with Sherman's foragers and would slit their throats, shoot or hang them before taking them prisoner. Sometimes they would leave desecrated bodies on the roadside with notes attached: "Death to all foragers." Sherman would retaliate, telling his commanders "shoot and leave by the roadside an equal number of prisoners and append a label on their bodies." [16]

Rumors about Sherman's march to the sea also struck fear in the North. For nearly three weeks, after Sherman had cut his communication lines in Atlanta, the only news about his march to Savannah had come from Southern newspapers. Their stories had proclaimed that Sherman's army had turned into a panic-stricken mob facing starvation and soon would surrender. Grant assured Washington officials that Sherman would reach "salt water." [17]

When Lincoln met Sherman and Grant aboard the steamer the River Queen in late March 1865, Lincoln listened to Sherman's stories about the march from Atlanta to Savannah and, in particular, about the exploits of the bummers. [18]

Before Sherman reached Savannah, Southern newspapers carried these dispatches. The *Augusta Sentinel*: "Yankee stragglers are being picked up. Where they have committed no improper act, they are treated as prisoners of war, but when it is ascertained that they have committed indecencies, they are shot." The *Augusta Constitution*: "Latest accounts represent Sherman's main body as vigorously passing through Millen." The *Augusta Sentinel*: "The advance has reached Millen. That settles the question that he is making direct for Savannah." [19]

Very few people actually knew where Sherman was heading, and his soldiers got a chuckle from the news stories. [20]

Before the fall of Atlanta, Sherman's army took a back seat in the Northern press as reporters followed Grant and the Army of the Potomac's battles with Confederate Gen. Robert E. Lee. When Atlanta fell, Sherman's troops began getting more coverage, and some Eastern soldiers in the Army of the Potomac became jealous because it seemed that story after story told of the success of Sherman's army of Westerners. [21] This competition between the two Union armies would resurface at the Grand Review.

Sherman's capture of Atlanta helped Lincoln to be re-elected in 1864. The President issued an order of national thanks to Sherman and his soldiers. [22]

Sherman's activities were hailed overseas, too. The *British Army and Navy Gazette* mused that if Sherman cut his supplies "and started off without a base to march from Georgia to South Carolina, he has done either one of the most brilliant or one of the most foolish things ever performed by a military leader." [23]

After leaving Georgia, Sherman planned to march through South and North Carolina and join Grant in Virginia, where they would help crush the seat of the rebellion.

Grant wanted Sherman to transport his soldiers north by ship, but Sherman convinced him that his soldiers wanted to march. Sherman and his army wanted to inflict as much pain as possible on South Carolina because they believed this state started the war. Sherman told Halleck, "I almost tremble at her fate but feel that she deserves all that seem in store for her." [24]

Sherman's psychological brand of warfare was working. Citizens and officials from Southern cities and towns shuddered when they learned that his army marched nearby. [25]

"The simple fact that a man's home has been visited by an enemy makes a soldier in Lee's or

Johnston's army very, very anxious to get home to look after his family and property," Sherman wrote to the Union commander in South Carolina.[26]

In Columbia, South Carolina, Sherman's army again made news. Fire had laid to waste a vast area of the capital of South Carolina. [27]

Southerners blamed Sherman for starting the fire. Sherman blamed Southerners.[28]

"I did not burn your town, nor did any of my army. Your brothers, sons, husbands and fathers set fire to the city, towns and villages in the land when they fired on Fort Sumter (in Charleston, South Carolina). The fire kindled then and thereby has been burning ever since and reached your houses last night." [29]

Meanwhile, the Union soldiers from the East finally began making strides against Robert E. Lee's Confederate troops at Petersburg, Virginia. Lee's army evacuated, and soon the boys from the East took Richmond, the capital of the Confed-eracy. Lee then began talks with Grant about a possible surrender.

Grant explained to Lincoln that he was "very anxious" to have the Union's Eastern armies push Lee from Richmond. He believed Sherman's army of Westerners would get all the credit if Cump's soldiers were anywhere near Richmond when

*USMHI*

Columbia, South Carolina,
after Sherman's army passed through.

Lee surrendered. It would have appeared that the Army of the Potomac could not defeat "the only army they had been engaged with," Grant said.

Lincoln told Grant he had not thought about that issue because he didn't care who crushed the rebellion, as long as the war ended.

Grant reported to the President and Stanton Lee's desire to surrender. Lincoln envisioned the end of the war. He proposed allowing Lee almost any terms, as long as the fighting stopped.[30]

Stanton listened and then interjected. "Mr. President, to-morrow is inauguration day. If you are not to be President of an obedient and united people, you had better not be inaugurated. If generals in the field are to negotiate peace, or any other chief magistrate is to be acknowledged on this continent, then you are not needed, and you had better not take the oath of office."

Lincoln considered this reasoning and told Stanton he was right. Lincoln wrote Grant on March 3, 1865, advising any talks with Lee be limited to military matters. The President, he confirmed, would handle any civil issues. "Now Stanton, date and sign this paper and send it to Grant," Lincoln said. "We'll see about this peace business." [31]

# Second Inaugural

## With Malice Toward None

## Someone Stop Johnson!

The next day, Lincoln took the oath for a second term and delivered his inaugural address aimed at healing the nation. "With malice toward none, with charity for all, with firmness in the right as God gives us to see the right, let us strive on to finish the work we are in, to bind up the nation's wounds. ..."

Before Lincoln spoke, Andrew Johnson, in his first public address as Vice President, delivered a speech that left people scratching their heads. A combination of sickness, nerves and alcohol caused him to lose the respect of the men he would lead just one month later.[1]

According to the *New York World*, Johnson began his speech commenting on the Constitution and remarking "what a striking thing it was." The *World* paraphrased Johnson, reporting he said "that it was the Constitution of the people of the country, and under it, here today, before the American Senate, he felt that he was a man and an American citizen."

Secretary of the Navy Welles called Johnson's speech rambling and strange.

As Johnson continued his wayward address, Attorney General James Speed leaned over and whispered to Welles, "All this is in wretched bad taste."

*ISHL*

Lincoln delivers his inaugural address.

Johnson continued to ramble, and Speed whispered to Welles again, "The man is certainly deranged."

The *World* reported that "Johnson would say to Senators and to others before him – to the Supreme Court, which sat before him, that they all got their power from the people of this country. Turning toward Mr. Chase, Mr. Johnson said: 'And your exaltation and position depend upon the people.' Turning toward the Cabinet, he said, 'And I will say to you, Mr. Secretary Seward, and to you Mr. Secretary Stanton, and to you, Mr. Secretary –' (To a gentleman nearby, sotto voice, 'Who is the Secretary of the Navy? The person addressed replied in a whisper, 'Mr. Welles') – 'and to you, Mr. Secretary Welles, I would say you derive your power from the people.'" Welles leaned over and told Stanton, who was sitting to his right, "Johnson is either drunk or crazy." Stanton replied, "There is evidently something wrong." [2]

*LC*

As outgoing Vice President Hannibal Hamlin read Johnson the oath, the Vice President-elect "stumbled, stammered, repeated portions of it several times over. The moment that he concluded this task, Mr. Johnson turned to the audience and commenced another speech, giving to those assembled his ideas of the oath which he had just taken," according to the *World*.

At one point, Johnson grabbed the Bible and in a booming voice declared: "I kiss this Book in the face of my nation of the United States." [3]

Johnson began to speak again, addressing the foreign ministers, "for he was going to tell the truth here today, that he was a plebeian and he thanked God for it." Johnson continued "when some of the officials standing near him had the good sense to stop him," the *World* reported.

Senator Zachariah Chandler of Michigan wrote to his wife, "I was never so mortified in my life. Had I been able to find a small hole, I should have dropped through it out of sight." [4]

Mary Todd Lincoln, the President's wife, would never forgive Johnson for embarrassing her husband on this grand occasion. [5]

The *World*'s March 5 headline summed up Johnson's speech: "The Most Incoherent Public Effort on Record."

# Section II

# The End of the War is in Sight

# President Lincoln in 1861

*LIA*

# President Lincoln in 1865

*LIA*

# Lee Surrenders to Grant

---

## Terms 'Magnanimous and Liberal'

---

## Stanton Offers His Resignation

On Palm Sunday, April, 9, 1865, at about 1:30 p.m., Gen. Lee and Gen. Grant met at the Wilmer McLean home in the village of Appomattox Court House, Virginia. Lee was about to surrender the Army of Northern Virginia.

After the two men exchanged greetings and small talk, Grant wrote terms of surrender based on a series of notes passed between the two generals in previous days. Grant's terms were lenient, as Lincoln desired. Lee signed the document. The two men talked for a short time and they parted ways.[1]

LIA

Lee signs Grant's terms of surrender.

The telegraph lines carried the news, and soon a dispatch appeared at the War Department. "General Lee surrendered the Army of Northern Virginia this afternoon upon terms proposed by myself. ... U.S. Grant, Lieutenant General." [2]

The Army of the Potomac celebrated, as did the people of the North. Grant ordered the army to begin its march back to Washington to be mustered out.

Sherman's army of Westerners rejoiced when it received the news. The men believed Lee would not surrender to Maj. Gen. George G. Meade's band of Easterners without their presence.[3] Sherman wrote Grant and congratulated him on his success. He also called Grant's terms "magnanimous and liberal" and said he would offer Confederate Gen. Joseph E. Johnston the same terms.[4]

In Washington, Stanton handed Lincoln his resignation, fulfilling his vow to resign at the end of the war. Lincoln ripped up the paper and embraced "The Great Energy."

"Stanton, you have been a good friend and a faithful public servant," Lincoln said, "and it is not for you to say when you will no longer be needed here." Stanton remained in his post.[5]

# Sherman and Johnston

# 'We Shall Have News Soon'

# Civil Authorities Want to Surrender

On April 14, 1865, at a cabinet meeting in Washington, Lincoln asked Grant if he had heard any news from Sherman. Grant told Lincoln he had not, but he was expecting news at any moment announcing the surrender of Joseph E. Johnston, the commander of the Army of Tennessee.

"Well," Lincoln told Grant, "you will hear very soon now, and the news will be important."

Grant asked the President how he knew. Lincoln explained he had a dream the previous night, "and ever since the war began, I have invariably had the same dream before any important military event occurred."

Welles asked Lincoln about his dream. "He said it related to the water, that he seemed to be on some singular, indescribable vessel and that he was moving with great rapidity," Welles said in his diary.

Lincoln told his cabinet that he had the same dream before the battles of Sumter, Bull Run, Antietam, Gettysburg, Stone River and Vicksburg. Grant interrupted the President to say that Stone River was no victory. Lincoln told Grant that the two may differ about the outcome, but, in any event, his dream preceded the battles.

Lincoln continued after Grant's interruption. "I had this strange dream again last night, and we shall, judging from the past, have great news very soon. I think it must be from Sherman. My thoughts are in that direction as are most of yours." [1]

LC

Gideon Welles

On April 14, Sherman received a letter from Johnston, the Confederate commander in the Western Theater, asking for a suspension of hostilities to "permit the civil authorities to enter into the needful arrangements to terminate the existing war." [2] Lincoln had been right. But the Johnston letter paled in importance to still another event that would occur on the same date.

Sherman was in Raleigh, North Carolina. He responded to Johnston and sent a telegram on April 15 to Washington. "I will accept the same terms as General Grant gave General Lee and be careful not to complicate any points of civil policy." [3]

The generals agreed to meet in Durham Station, North Carolina, on April 17. As Sherman and his officers boarded the train for the 26-mile trip, he was handed a shocking message from Stanton. [4] President Lincoln had been assassinated on April 14, Good Friday. He had died the next day. Stanton said the assassins attempted to kill Secretary of State William H. Seward and warned Sherman his life also was in danger. Sherman told the messenger not to tell anyone, for he feared his soldiers' reaction.[5]

At the James Bennett farmhouse, Johnston and Sherman sat at a small wooden table. Their staff officers remained outside, leaving the generals to meet in private. The two generals had never met, but each knew of the other's battle strategies. Both had graduated from West Point. "Old Joe," as Johnston was called by his soldiers, was 13 years Sherman's senior.[6]

Sherman showed Johnston Stanton's telegram and watched as beads of sweat formed on the Confederate's head. Johnston could only reply that Lincoln was the best friend that Southerners had.[7]

"Friendly" did not describe the relationship between Johnston and Confederate President Jefferson Davis, who had removed Johnston from command in July 1864 because of his inability to stop Sherman in Atlanta.[8] The Confederate government had believed that if the Union could not win any substantial battles before the 1864 elections, Northern-

USMHI

Above, Johnston greets Sherman at the Bennett farmhouse.

Below, the staffs of Johnston and Sherman talk about the war outside the farmhouse.

USMHI

ers would support the Peace Democrats at the voting booths, sweep Lincoln from office, and the South's separate government would be secured.[9]

Johnston, who had commanded the Confederate army at war's outset, had left his command a dejected officer. He joined his family in Macon, Georgia. To replace Johnston, Davis turned to John B. Hood, who later resigned, in January 1865, after three major defeats.[10]

To increase the morale of Southern soldiers, the Confederate Congress quickly appointed Lee as general-in-chief of the Confederate army and assigned Johnston to the command of the Army of Tennessee. Davis supported Lee's appointment but refused to restore Johnston to command. Lee also refused.[11]

In February 1865, a reluctant Davis restored Johnston to command. But "Old Joe" became suspicious, believing he would be the scapegoat if the Confederacy collapsed.[12]

The next month, Johnston was called to meet Davis and members of his cabinet in Greensboro,

North Carolina. At the time, Johnston was unaware Lee had surrendered. He learned of it at Greensboro.[13]

At the meeting, Davis tried to rally his leaders.

"I think we can whip the enemy yet, if our people will turn out," he said. "We must look at matters calmly. Whatever can be done must be done at once."

After a pause, Davis asked Johnston for his thoughts.

"My views are, sir, that our people are tired of the war. My men are deserting in large numbers and are taking my artillery teams to aid their escape to their homes. Since Lee's defeat they regard the war as at an end."

Johnston concluded by saying, "We may, perhaps, obtain terms which we ought to accept."

Davis sat, his eyes transfixed on a scrap of paper. He listened as others in the room agreed with Johnston. Davis asked Johnston how he proposed to obtain the terms because the "enemy refuses to treat with us." Johnston said he could arrange a meeting with Sherman. Davis dictated a letter to Sherman, and Johnston signed it. [14]

So, at the Bennett farmhouse, where Johnston and Sherman met, "Old Joe" sat in front of Cump intent on arranging a permanent peace that would involve the governments of the two armies. For some reason, Sherman misunderstood Johnston's initial letter, in which he clearly stated a peace of "civil authorities." When Johnston explained his surrender position, Sherman called it impossible because the Union did not recognize the Confederate government. Sherman then offered Johnston the same terms Lee had accepted.[15]

Johnston listened and then enticed Sherman by suggesting they "make one job of it" by settling "the fate of all armies to the Rio Grande." [16]

Sherman asked Johnston if he had such authority. Johnston said Confederate Secretary of War John C. Breckinridge was nearby and could speak for the government.[17] Sherman knew he might be overstepping his bounds if he talked to a member of the Confederate government. But Johnston reminded Sherman that Breckinridge was also a general in the Confederate army.[18] Sherman told Johnston the three should meet the next day.[19]

Sherman returned to Raleigh and told his soldiers of Lincoln's assassination. His army wanted to burn the city, but Sherman ordered his troops not to retaliate.[20]

The next day, Sherman met Johnston and Breckinridge at the Bennett farmhouse. To break the ice, Sherman offered the two men a drink of bourbon. Breckinridge, who had been Vice President of the United States in 1857, perked up at the offer. He tossed out his plug of tobacco, rinsed out his month and poured himself a generous drink. He tossed it down and then began to rattle off laws and suggestions for the surrender terms. Sherman shot back, "See here, gentlemen, who is doing the surrendering anyhow? If this thing goes on, you'll have me sending an apology to Jeff Davis." [21]

A messenger arrived with a letter from Confederate Postmaster-General John H. Reagan suggesting more surrender terms.[22] Sherman refused them. He then began writing terms based on his conversations with Lincoln while on the River Queen in March. Lincoln had simply wanted the war to end with the Union intact.[23]

But Sherman also wanted terms that would reduce any likelihood of Confederate soldiers breaking up into "guerrilla bands."

"Such men as Wade Hampton, (Nathan Bedford) Forrest, Wirt Adams, etc., never will work and nothing is left for them but death or highway robbery," Sherman explained to his wife, Ellen. "They will not work and their negroes are all gone, their plantations destroyed, etc. I will be glad if I can open a way for them abroad." [24]

While deep in thought, Sherman stood, retrieved the bourbon from his saddlebag and poured himself another drink as Johnston and Breckinridge watched. He returned to the table and finished the document. [25]

Sherman told the two Confederates the terms must be approved in Washington before they could become official. Sherman's terms, unlike Grant's, established peace from the Potomac to the Rio Grande, but they also allowed Southern states many of the same comforts they enjoyed before the Civil War, including the possibility to restore slavery. His

*USMHI*

Sherman reviews the surrender terms.
Johnston, sitting, watches.

terms also posed the possibility of the federal government assuming the South's war debt. Some believed Sherman's terms were nothing more than an edited version of Confederate Reagan's suggestions. In his memoirs, Sherman maintained he penned the document himself. Whatever the case, Johnston signed it.[26]

When the two Confederates left Sherman, Johnston asked Breckinridge his thoughts about the Union general. Breckinridge commented on Sherman's abilities and added a personal observation.

*LIA*

John C. Breckinridge

"General Sherman is a hog. Yes sir, a hog. Did you see him take that drink by himself? No Kentucky gentleman would ever have taken away that bottle." [27]

Proudly, Sherman proclaimed to his commanders that Washington would approve his terms. Before government officials even reviewed them, Sherman had issued Special Orders No. 58, in which he described "an agreement with General Johnston and high officials which, when formally ratified, will make peace from the Potomac to the Rio Grande ... and the General hopes and believes that in a very few days it will be his good fortune to conduct you all to your homes." [28]

Sherman wrote his wife, Ellen, "I can hardly realize it, but I can see no slip. The terms are all on our side." [29]

He wrote and asked his friend Halleck to use his influence in Washington to push the terms through, "for I have considered everything." [30]

Once again, Sherman believed himself the victor. He had penned terms of surrender that, if approved, would end the war. What he did not know was that an excited and anxious Stanton was running the government after Lincoln's assassination.

# Terms Denied

## Stanton Prepares for Battle

## Has Sherman Gone Mad?

Sherman's terms created an immediate buzz when they reached Washington on April 21, 1865. Grant read the document and knew immediately that Sherman's terms would not be approved. He quickly sent a copy to Stanton, who advised President Johnson to call a meeting of the cabinet. The meeting was set for 8 p.m.[1]

These were extremely difficult days. Lincoln's body was moving slowly toward Springfield, Illinois; Secretary Seward remained at home, suffering from the knife wound of a would-be assassin; guards stood at the homes of important politicians; the Secret Service and portions of the army searched for Jefferson Davis and hunted Lincoln's assassin, John Wilkes Booth. This was no time for surprises.

At the War Department, before the cabinet meeting, Stanton prepared to wage a personal war with Sherman. He dictated to David Homer Bates, manager of the War Department's telegraph office, a response to Sherman's terms.

*USMHI*

Lincoln's funeral procession in Chicago.

"Although as a telegrapher I was a rapid penman, my task was not an easy one, for the great War Secretary's sentences came tumbling from his lips in an impetuous torrent and it was impossible for me to keep up the pace he set," Bates later related. "I did my best, but lost some words and transposed others, so that the fiery dictator was forced to go back several times in his train of thought and reconstruct sentences, and in doing so here and there he used phrases different from those in his original composition."

An angry Stanton snatched the paper from Bates' hand and berated him for what he thought was an unsatisfactory job.

"Taking a pen in his hand and dipping it vigorously into the inkstand he proceeded to rewrite a considerable part of the document himself," Bates said of Stanton. "He read it over to me carefully and then had me write a new copy entire, while he paced back and forth across the room impatient of the fast-speeding minutes, and occasionally looking over my shoulder to see how far I had progressed."

When Bates finished, he handed the copy to Stanton, who walked away. Stanton later apologized for his actions.

"I was too hasty with you, Mr. Bates. The fault was mine in expecting you to keep up with my rapid dictation; but I was so indignant at General Sherman for having presumed to enter into such an arrangement with the enemy, that I forgot everything else." [2]

At the cabinet meeting, Grant read the communication from Sherman. President Johnson and his cabinet listened and flatly refused Sherman's terms to a man. Stanton counted off on his fingers reasons the terms had to be rejected.[3]

David Homer Bates

Once again, as in Kentucky at the beginning of the war, Sherman's mental capabilities were being questioned. Stanton's private secretary, Maj. Albert E.H. Johnson, told Bates that President Johnson said the terms were "close to treason" and called Sherman a traitor. Grant agreed with refusing the terms, but he did not berate Sherman, Welles said.[4] Grant was sent to North Carolina to take control of Sherman's army in Raleigh. In the name of the President, Stanton virtually had removed Sherman from command.[5]

Stanton told Grant, "No one of any class or shade of opinion approves it. I have not known as much surprise and discontent at anything that has happened during the war. ... The hope of the country is that you may repair the misfortune occasioned by Sherman's negotiations."[6]

Stanton launched a public attack on Sherman. The Secretary of War fired a statement to the press in the form of a letter to Gen. John A. Dix in which he listed "nine reasons" why Sherman's terms were not approved. Stanton believed that if he hesitated at rebuking Sherman, the Republican Party would lose everything it had gained with the North's victory. Stanton knew the Democrats had great interest in Sherman, and the Copperhead Party wanted to elevate the popular general to the White House.[7]

Washington was in a frenzy, and the press leaped on the story. The great Sherman had blundered.

LC

Attorney General
James Speed

When news of Sherman's terms and Stanton's "nine reasons" hit the New York Sunday papers, members of the cabinet started to panic. Attorney General Speed, prompted by Stanton, expressed fears that Sherman wanted to take over the government. By Tuesday, the cabinet's discussion of Sherman became more frantic. Speed arrived at the cabinet meeting charged, saying Sherman "was designing to put himself at the head of the army." Speed said Sherman had been seduced by Breckinridge and thought he would be able to control and direct public affairs.

"Suppose," Speed said, "he should arrest Grant when Grant arrived at Raleigh." [8]

Sherman's friend Halleck added to the frenzy when he reported that the Confederate President had left Richmond with a large amount of gold and other valuables. Halleck, now stationed in Richmond, suggested that Sherman may have aided Davis' escape when he ordered one of his officers away from the Confederate's planned route.[9] All this was played out in newspapers. Editorial writers questioned Sherman's motives and politicians questioned his sanity. Sherman, at the time, had no knowledge of any of it.[10]

This wasn't the first time Sherman had felt the bite of the national press. A previous experience also involved a Secretary of War.

Near the beginning of the war in 1861, Sherman had believed the citizens of Kentucky, one of four Southern states that did not secede from the Union, could not be trusted to fight against the Confederates.[11]

When an ailing Secretary of War Simon Cameron of Harrisburg, Pennsylvania, arrived in Kentucky in October with his entourage, he met a stressed Sherman who sought a private meeting. The Secretary of War assured Sherman that the people in the room were close friends.[12]

Sherman locked the door and turned to Cameron, announcing he needed at least 60,000 men to protect Kentucky and 200,000 more to take the war to the Confederates. Lying on Sherman's bed, Cameron protested, "You astonish me. Great God ... where are they to come from?" Draft Northerners who want to fight, Sherman retorted.[13]

Unbeknownst to Sherman, at least one of Cameron's "close friends" was a newspaper reporter.[14]

Sherman wanted to leave Kentucky because he believed he would not receive any additional military support. "I am to be sacrificed," he stated.[15]

By November 1861, Sherman had joined Halleck, who was stationed in St. Louis at the time. Halleck ordered Sherman to have a physical examination. The doctor declared Sherman "unfit for command," and Halleck persuaded his friend to take a 20-day leave. A dejected Cump went home to his wife in Lancaster, Ohio.[16]

Meanwhile, Halleck wrote to Gen. George McClellan, the Union commander in 1861, to say Sherman was a broken man.[17]

Then the insults began. On Dec. 11, 1861, the headline in the *Cincinnati Commercial* read "General William T. Sherman Insane." The story related, "It appears that he was at the time while commanding in Kentucky, stark mad." Other newspapers reprinted the *Commercial* story. In *Frank Leslie's Illustrated Newspaper*, two sentences under the headline "Personal" explained Sherman's action: "General Sherman, who lately commanded in Kentucky, is said to be insane. It is charitable to think so."

Sherman's family wanted him to file a lawsuit claiming libel.[18] His brother, Sen. John Sherman, and Halleck discouraged the idea. In his memoirs, John Sherman said Cameron denied starting the insanity gossip.[19]

After Sherman was restored to duty, he wrote his brother John in January 1862, "I should have committed suicide were it not for my children. I don't think I can again be entrusted with command." [20]

When Grant, following orders to correct Cump's negotiations "folly," arrived in North Carolina, he slipped unnoticed into Sherman's headquarters, intent on allowing Sherman to re-negotiate the surrender terms with Johnston. Sherman was surprised to see Grant and listened as his "sworn friend" explained why the government denied his truce with Johnston. Grant suggested that Sherman offer Johnston the same terms Lee had accepted. Sherman heeded Grant's wishes.[21] He contacted Johnston, and the two men met at the Bennett farmhouse for a third and final time on April 26, 1865. Johnston signed the terms and the two men parted. Grant returned to Washington, and Sherman believed the matter was "surely at an end." [22]

Two days later, Sherman realized the mess he had caused when he read the April 24 edition of the *New York Times*. The headlines on the front page rang: "Sherman's Action Promptly Repudiated," and "The President and All His Cabinet Rebuke Him," and "Gen. Grant Gone to North Carolina to Direct Our Armies." After seeing the headlines, Sherman read Stanton's "nine reasons" and Halleck's suggestion that Sherman aided Jefferson Davis' escape to Mexico or Europe with as much as $13 million in plunder. He read Stanton's comments about the March 3, 1865, order from Lincoln to Grant, in which the President told Grant not to deal with any civil matters when talking to Lee. Sherman flew into a rage. He had never been told of Lincoln's order. [23]

A general who was present when Sherman lashed out at Stanton said Cump paced the floor like a "caged lion" calling Stanton "a mean, scheming, vindictive politician who made it his business to rob military men of the credit earned by exposing their lives." [24]

Anyone who would listen heard Sherman rail against Washington. In his opinion, he had only followed Lincoln's wishes.

In an April 25 letter to Stanton, Sherman softened his rhetoric. He wrote, "I admit my folly in embracing in a military convention any civil matters." But he put the Secretary of War on the spot by saying he was following Stanton's wishes: In Savannah, Stanton had confided in Sherman that the war must end quickly because he feared it would bankrupt the government. [26]

Sherman wrote to Grant on April 28 defending his position. [27] He had the right as a field officer to make terms, and he and Johnston knew Washington's approval was necessary before they became official. He said Stanton violated the secrecy of military communications and allowed the dogs of "the press to be let loose upon me." [28]

In May, Sherman returned to Savannah on business. [29] On his return to Raleigh, Sherman's steamer, the Russia, became stranded in North Carolina because of bad weather. He began reading the New York newspapers, and again the words tore into him like bullets. He wrote home to his wife, "I have seen the New York papers of April 24 and 28, but don't mind them much, for it is manifest that some deviltry is on foot." [30] Despite the tone of Sherman's letter home, he must have reeled from the words spoken by historian George Bancroft when Lincoln's funeral procession stopped in New York City. The newspapers of April 28 reported that Bancroft told the crowd that Sherman had seized more power than the president "and has revived slavery and given security and political power to traitors from the Chesapeake to the Rio Grande."

Even Sherman's supportive brother John, the Senator, thought Cump's terms odd. In a letter to Stanton, he said, "I am distressed beyond measure at the terms granted to Johnston by General Sherman. They are inadmissible." Sherman's wife, Ellen, also thought the terms too soft.

"News electrified us on Monday (April 24) of your mild terms to Joe Johnston," Ellen wrote to her husband. "You know me well enough to realize that I would never agree to any such policies as that towards deserters from our Union." [31]

The New York Times articles questioning his sanity angered Sherman. One story asked, "Has Sherman gone mad?" The London Times hinted that Sherman had ambition to be a dictator. The Cincinnati Commercial reported he had been bamboozled by the Confederates at the Bennett farmhouse. But the story that caused the most pain involved his friend Halleck. Sherman read that "Old Brains" Halleck had directed Sherman's men to disregard his truce and told officers "Obey no orders of General Sherman." Halleck also sent soldiers from the Army of the Potomac to cut any possible retreat by Johnston's army. This was an insult to Sherman. Grant intervened for he knew Halleck's order would offend Sherman. Grant informed Halleck that Johnston had accepted the same terms given to Lee, and asked Halleck to "Please order [Philip] Sheridan back to Petersburg at once." [32]

A betrayed Sherman began to feel his only friends were soldiers and the people of the South. In a

*USMHI*

Chief Justice
Salmon P. Chase

May 6 letter to Supreme Court Justice Chase, Lincoln's former Secretary of the Treasury, Sherman said he knew the Southern people. "I have no fear of them armed or disarmed ... and, in war, would not hesitate to mingle with them and lead them to battle against a national foe." [33]

Thoughts of leaving the military raced through Sherman's mind.[34] Chase persuaded Sherman to stay on. Chase told him the problems in Washington could be traced to the "assassination of Mr. Lincoln, the sudden ascension to power of Mr. Johnson, who was supposed to be bitter and vindictive in his feelings toward the South, and the wild pressure of every class of politicians to enforce on the new president their pet schemes." [35]

On May 6, Sherman explained to his army in Special Orders No. 69 what was happening. He said "a most foul attempt" had been made on his fame. The insults were personal and did not reflect upon his soldiers. He asked his army to "restrain their feelings when they come in Contact with their Comrades in Virginia." Sherman promised revenge: "The parties who instigated this base attempt are yet unknown, but will be discovered and properly punished." [36]

Sherman told Chase he believed this special order would "lead to the closing of my military career." [37] Sherman was losing his edge. The man who had marched his army through more than 1,000 miles of hostile territory and received national thanks after Atlanta's fall began to question his authority. When Maj. Gen. John M. Schofield telegraphed Sherman about Schofield being considered for military governor of North Carolina, Cump said he would back Schofield "with my influence, which, however, cannot amount to much in the present attitude of affairs." [38]

The war was over, but Sherman began another battle, this time to regain his honor. As he wrote his wife on May 8, "I am not dead yet by a long sight and those matters give me new life for I see the Cause." [39]

In his memoirs, Sherman did not suppress his feelings.

"To say that I was angry at the tone and substance of these published bulletins of the War Department would hardly express the state of my feelings. I was outraged beyond measure, and was resolved to resent the insult, cost what it might." [40]

# Return to Richmond

## The Nerve of Halleck

## Stanton Wants to Kill Me

While Sherman was away, his soldiers in North Carolina received orders to march to Richmond en route to Washington to be released from the military and sent home. Many of the soldiers were upset about the treatment of Uncle Billy, but their anger raged over what was happening to them.[1]

Rumors circulated among the soldiers that some officers had bet on whose men would reach Richmond first. This march was one of the most grueling Sherman's army had experienced. Thousands struggled through the brutal heat and humidity of North Carolina and Virginia. Hundreds became ill and some died.

"This brutality should be investigated," one soldier complained.[2]

"We have never made a much harder march and some of our Generals deserved to have their necks broke for such 'Tom foolery' after the war," another soldier ranted.[3]

When Sherman stopped at Fort Monroe in Virginia en route to his army, he received a letter dated May 8 from Halleck. "When you arrive here come directly to my headquarters. I have a room for you and will have rooms elsewhere for your staff."[4]

The nerve of Halleck, Sherman thought. Only seven months before, after the fall of Atlanta in September 1864, Sherman must have warmed Halleck's heart when he thanked "Old Brains" for "all I now enjoy of fame." He said Halleck helped him through the period when he was being called insane and "gradually put me in the way of recovering from what might have proven an ignoble end."[5]

But now Halleck was the enemy. Sherman returned a pointed letter the same day. "After your dispatch to the Secretary of War of April 26th I cannot have any friendly intercourse with you. I will come to City Point tomorrow and march with my troops and I prefer we should not meet."[6]

When he reached the outskirts of Richmond on May 9, Sherman found his troops in an uproar. They were not allowed to enter the city, even though Eastern soldiers had access. Some soldiers wanted to shoot their way into the city.[7]

Then Halleck tore open Sherman's wound when he ordered Jefferson C. Davis' 14th Corps into the city to march in review.[8] Of all the audacity!

"This I forbade," Sherman wrote his wife.[9]

"All the army knew of the insult that had been made me by the Secretary of War and General Halleck, and watched me closely to see if I would tamely submit," Sherman said in his memoirs.[10]

Sherman was in limbo. Was he still in command of his officers? Halleck, with Stanton's approval, had told Sherman's commanders not to obey any of Cump's orders. Sherman turned to Grant. "Does the Secretary of War's newspaper order take Wilson from my command or shall I continue to order him? If I have proven incompetent to manage my own command let me know it." [11]

While waiting for Grant's reply, Sherman wrote to Schofield. "In a day or so I will hear from General Grant whether I am to command my own subordinates or not." Grant responded on May 9: "I know of no order which changes your command in any particular." Sherman was still in command. [12]

Maj. Gen. John Schofield

In a May 9 letter to Halleck, Sherman showed that his confidence had returned and he was ready to trade insult for insult. Sherman had regained control of his loyal soldiers. He told "Old Brains" he would march his army through Richmond only when Grant issued the order. Damn what Halleck thought! As for the review ordered by Halleck, Sherman told him it "will not take place." [13]

Halleck attempted to smooth things over by professing great friendship for Sherman. "You have not had during this war nor have you now a warmer friend and admirer than myself," Halleck wrote in a May 10 telegraph. "If in carrying out what I knew to be the wishes of the War Department in regard to your armistice I used language which has given you offense it was unintentional, and I deeply regret it." [14]

The same day he was professing a kinship with Sherman, Halleck telegraphed Stanton, withdrawing his recommendation of Schofield as military governor of North Carolina. His reason: "It is represented to me that (Schofield) and General (Frank) Blair were the principal advisers of Sherman in his armistice with the rebel General Johnston. If so, he is not a proper person to command in North Carolina." [15]

Halleck's "friendship letter" did not assuage Sherman, who responded the same day with a warning to "Old Brains." "If noticed by some of my old command I cannot undertake to maintain a model behavior, for their feelings have become aroused," Sherman wrote. "If loss of life or violence result from this you must attribute it to the true cause — a public insult to a brother officer when he was far away on public service." [16]

Sherman confided in a May 10 letter to Ellen, "All the officers and men have been to see me in camp to-day and they received with shouts my public denial of a review for Halleck. ... I dare him to oppose my march. He will think twice before he again undertakes to stand between me and my subordinates." [17]

Meanwhile, on May 10, Confederate President Davis was captured in Irwinville, Georgia, with some members of his cabinet and his family. In his possession was only about $500,000, not the $6 million to $13 million in gold and valuables Halleck claimed Davis had taken. [18]

In a May 10 letter to Grant marked "Confidential," Sherman spilled out his disdain for Halleck and Stanton and warned his "sworn friend:" "He [Stanton] seeks your life and reputation as well as mine. Beware, but you are Cool and have been most skillful in managing such People, and I have faith you will penetrate his designs. He wants the vast patronage of the military Governorships of the South, and the votes of the Free Negro loyal citizens for political Capital, and whoever stands in his way must die."

Sherman told Grant to "keep above such influences, or you will also be a victim. See in my case how soon all past services are ignored & forgotten. Excuse this letter. Burn it, but heed my friendly counsel. The lust for Power in political Minds is the strongest passion of Life, and impels Ambitious Men (Richard III) to deeds of Infamy." [19]

After Grant gave the order, Sherman's army marched defiantly through Richmond on May 11, 1865, en route to Washington.[20] The streets were lined with citizens and Eastern soldiers, some in white collars, who shouted insults at Sherman's army, calling them "slouch hats" and "Sherman's greasers," and bragged that the Westerners never had to tangle with Robert E. Lee. Some of Sherman's troops volleyed insults of their own at the Eastern soldiers: "All quiet on the Potomac." At Halleck's headquarters, one of Sherman's soldiers broke ranks and spat a stream of tobacco juice on the polished boots of a guard. Halleck watched from his portico as Sherman and his men marched by. Not one soldier offered Halleck his due — the military salute of respect.[21]

Sherman vented his anger about the treatment of his men at Richmond in a May 12 letter to Gen. John "Black Jack" Logan. Sherman said Halleck's welcome "was a part of a

*LC*

Maj. Gen. Henry W. Halleck

grand game to insult us — us who have marched 1,000 miles through a hostile country in mid-winter to help them. We did help them and what has been our reward?" Sherman continued by saying Halleck allowed citizens, "rebels of course," to come and go, but not his soldiers. "If such be the welcome the East gives the West, we can but let them make war and fight it out themselves." [22]

In a letter to Ellen, Sherman wrote how he treated Halleck and hinted at what was in store for Stanton.

"Unless Grant interposes from his yielding and good nature I shall get some equally good opportunity to insult Stanton," Sherman said. "Stanton wants to kill me because I do not favor the scheme of declaring the negroes of the South, now free, to be loyal voters." [23]

# Time to Go Home

---

## Troops Arrive in Washington

---

## The Eve of the Grand Review

As they marched toward Alexandria, Virginia, Sherman and his troops surveyed the battlefields where the Eastern army had clashed with Lee's army. Many were unimpressed. Some believed their march through the South left marks of a much greater struggle.[1] Sherman shifted from column to column to see as much as he could of the aftermath. He visited Hanover Court House, Spotsylvania, Fredericksburg and Dumfries, among other sites. In Petersburg and Richmond, the battlefields remained fresh from the fighting and the evils of war were apparent.[2]

*USMHI*

Richmond, Virginia, left in ruins.

By May 17, Sherman and his army made camp near Alexandria. The conditions were sloppy, and the men wanted a new site. They were dirty, insulted and irritable over their reception in Richmond and having gone unpaid for nearly 10 months.[3]

While in camp, Sherman maintained the tone that would shroud the Grand Review.

"Tell (the) newspaper(s) that the Vandal Sherman is encamped near the Canal bridge half way between the Long Bridge & Alexandria to the west of the road, where his friends if any can find him," Sherman said. "Though in disgrace, he is untamed & unconquered." [4]

Rumors circulated through Washington that Sherman and his loyal army planned to take over the government. Gossip spread with Sherman's pronouncement, published in the *New York Times*, that he would not enter Washington without orders from the President or Grant. The headline read: "Gen. Sherman Does not Care to Visit Washington."

Sherman's attitude was a hot topic of discussion in Washington. His family worried he might do something rash. The Committee on the Conduct of War called him to testify.

Grant wrote Sherman on May 19 asking him to visit and speak "upon matters about which you feel sore." [5]

Grant knew of Sherman's pain. He, too, had been victimized by Halleck — twice in three months in 1862.

In early March 1862, Halleck, Grant's superior at the time, had suggested Grant be removed from command after his victory at Fort Donelson.

Halleck had written Gen. George McClellan saying Grant had refused to supply him with field reports. "Old Brains" also said Grant had gone to Nashville without authorization. [6] Halleck even brought up the issue of Grant's perceived fondness of alcohol. This was done without Grant's knowledge by a man who Grant thought was his friend. [7]

"A rumor has just reached me that since the taking of Fort Donelson General Grant has resumed his former bad habits," Halleck told McClellan. [8]

McClellan relieved Grant from duty and ordered an investigation into charges against him. McClellan authorized Grant's arrest. [9]

"Thus in less than two weeks after the victory at Donelson, the two leading generals in the army were in correspondence as to what disposition should be made of me, and in less than three weeks I was virtually in arrest and without a command," Grant said. [10]

No investigation occurred, and Grant was restored to command on March 13, 1862. [11]

Grant's second run-in with Halleck had occurred in May 1862 at Corinth, Mississippi. Halleck had sent orders to Grant's commanders without allowing Grant to see them.

"Orders were sent direct to the right wing or reserve, ignoring me, and advances were made from one line of intrenchments to another without notifying me. My position was so embarrassing in fact that I made several applications during the siege to be relieved," Grant said later. [12]

At one point, Grant had suggested to Halleck a possible plan of action. "I was silenced so quickly that I felt that possibly I had suggested an unmilitary movement," he said. [13]

"My position at Corinth, with a nominal command and yet no command, became so unbearable that I asked permission of Halleck to remove my headquarters to Memphis. I had repeatedly asked, between the fall of Donelson and the evacuation of Corinth, to be relieved from duty under Halleck; but all my applications were refused until the occupation of the town. I then obtained permission to leave the department, but General Sherman happened to call on me as I was about starting and urged me so strongly not to think of going, that I concluded to remain." [14]

In a letter to his wife, Sherman explained the moment: "I have stood by Grant in his days of sorrow. He sat in his tent almost weeping at the accumulated charges against him. He had made up his mind to leave for good. I begged him, and he yielded. I could see his good points and his weak points better than I could my own, and he now feels I stood by him in his days of dejection and he is my sworn friend." [15]

True to his word, Sherman entered Washington only after he received an invitation from President Johnson and Gen. Grant. [16] In the nation's capital, Sherman saw guards posted at the homes of government officials, including Stanton's, something he viewed as unnecessary. When Johnson met Sherman, the President thanked Cump for coming. He assured Sherman that Stanton acted alone in publishing the report on the general's truce with Johnston. Other cabinet members also assured Sherman that they were not involved. [17]

Grant asked Sherman to reconcile with Stanton. Sherman flatly refused. "Mr. Stanton can give me no orders of himself. No man shall insult me with impunity. ... Subordination to Authority is one thing, to insult Another. Mr. Stanton must publicly confess himself a public libeler or — but I won't threaten." [18]

On May 18, 1865, Grant issued Special Orders No. 239, announcing that the Grand Review of the

Union armies would take place on Tuesday, May 23, and Wednesday, May 24. Only soldiers who had fought in the four-year war could participate. All bars and saloons were ordered closed from 6 a.m. Monday to 10 p.m. Wednesday.[19]

Grant was asked why the event would take two days. According to newspaper accounts, Grant said, "It will consume two entire days to pass the army across the Long Bridge," adding that "if the same army were moving against the enemy, with all its trains, in ordinary marching order, the line would reach from Washington to Richmond."

Originally, Stanton wanted the entire Union army, more than 1 million soldiers, in Washington for the Grand Review.[20] During the war, Stanton had read voraciously the British magazines that predicted the Union could not be preserved and the peace of Europe would be safer with two or three republics in America instead of one. These stories rang constantly in Stanton's ears.[21] On these two days in May, he envisioned an opportunity to display to the world the fighting spirit of America and the strength of her armies and military equipment. He knew foreign representatives would be present and the event would be reported in journals from London to Paris and from Mexico to Saint Petersburg. But the cost of transporting soldiers and equipment forced him to change his mind.[22]

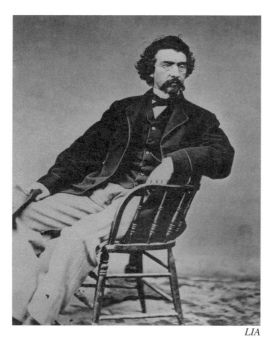

LIA

Photographer Mathew Brady

By Sunday, May 21, crowds began descending on the capital. A *New York Times* article of May 22 described the crowded trains and hordes of spectators, and then noted, "and to crown all, [Mathew] Brady, the photographer of New York, has his arrangements all complete for copying the pageant and handing it down to posterity, in the highest style of art."

The *New York Times* published a front-page story on May 23 that predicted, "Few people will have the patience to gaze for seven or eight long hours in the hot sun at the never-ending stream of troops that will pour through the city to-morrow." How wrong that reporter was. Thousands upon thousands of people from near and far came to Washington to witness the Grand Review. Never had the nation's capital seen such throngs. More people viewed the Grand Review than witnessed Lincoln's first or second inaugural or his funeral procession.[23]

Sherman and other officers sent word home, encouraging their families to attend.

With every hotel full, visitors accepted any type of accommodations. Some paid locals to stay in unused rooms. Those who could not find lodging inside a building camped in the streets.

In and around Washington, the campsites of soldiers dotted fields and woods. Rows of white tents stretched as far as the eye could see. Curious civilians could venture into these camps and witness army life first-hand.[24]

In front of the Executive Mansion, laborers had begun building reviewing stands. Special tickets allowed 200 select spectators to view the event in style from the two main reviewing stands on Pennsylvania Avenue.

Stand No. 1 was for the President, members of his cabinet, the reviewing officers, heads of civil and military departments and the diplomatic corps. Stand No. 2 was reserved for governors, members of Congress and judges. A wealthy man from Boston, John M. Forbes, paid to have stands No. 3 and 4 built for wounded and disabled veterans from Washington hospitals. Generals of the army and admirals and commodores of the navy and members of the press were to be accommodated as well as possible on the latter two stands. [25]

Soldiers were getting ready to march. Meade wrote to Grant that the armies should be allowed to "cadence" step from the Capitol to the President's home. "I think both the officers and men deserve it," he said. Grant agreed.[26]

Meanwhile, the Committee on the Conduct of War wanted to hear from Sherman. Originally, he was to appear after the Grand Review. But with rumors swirling, he was called to testify the day before the event.[27]

Members wanted to know the reasoning behind Sherman's surrender terms with Johnston, among other things. Sherman remained defiant as he presented his case. The inquisition went on for hours and at one point Sherman stated to the committee, "And it does seem strange to me that every bar-room loafer in New York can read in the morning journals official matter that is withheld from a general whose command extends from Kentucky to North Carolina." [28]

Sherman's anger did not wane as he related how he was treated by Stanton and Halleck.

"I did feel indignant — I do feel indignant. As to my own honor, I can protect it," Sherman said. "Had President Lincoln lived, I know he would have sustained me." [29]

Sherman's family intervened, worried that he might do something foolish. Sherman had written on May 10 to his wife, "They will find that Sherman who was not scared by the Crags of Lookout, the Barriers of Kenesaw, and (the) long and trackless forests of the South is not to be intimidated by the howlings of a set of sneaks who were hid away as long as danger was rampant, but now shriek with very courage. I will take a Regiment of my old Division & clear them all out." [30]

*LC*

Sen. John Sherman

Sherman's brother-in-law, Hugh Boyle Ewing, was so concerned he pulled John Sherman out of a barber chair at Willard's Hotel and took him and another family member to Charles Sherman's room for a hastily called strategy session. They chose John Sherman to talk sense into Cump.[31]

On the eve of the Grand Review, John and Cump Sherman walked on Pennsylvania Avenue near the Capitol. No doubt, their conversation involved Halleck and Secretary of War Stanton — John Sherman's next-door neighbor.

As the two men talked, someone on the crowded street recognized the general, and soon a crush of admirers pressed against the brothers. They shook Cump's hand and cheered him. Women waved handkerchiefs. Among the Northern public, Sherman was second only to Grant in popularity. Sherman quickly hailed a carriage and the hack spirited the two brothers away.[32]

Photographer Mathew Brady used the days leading up to the Grand Review as an opportunity to photograph the Union soldiers. The prized picture for Brady would be of Sherman and his staff.

When the photographer found Sherman at Willard's Hotel, Cump said he would pose with his staff, "but all my officers are away with their wives, children and sweethearts. It is impossible to get them together, Mr. Brady."

Brady asked Sherman, "If I find them and gather them together at my gallery at two o'clock tomorrow, will you be there?"

Sherman laughed and told Brady that if he could locate the officers he would pose for a picture.

Brady, with the help of his aides, found all of Sherman's staff and sent Cump a note. Sherman replied he would attend.

When Sherman and his commanders arrived at Brady's studio, they had to wait for a tardy Maj.

*USMHI*

Sherman poses with his staff at Brady's studio. Sitting left to right are John A. Logan, Sherman and Henry W. Slocum. Standing left to right are O.O. Howard, William B. Hazen, Jefferson C. Davis and Joseph A. Mower. Frank Blair is missing.

*USMHI*

In this picture, Blair is photographed with the group. He is seated on the right.

Gen. Frank Blair. At one point, the door opened and a young woman and her 3-year-old daughter stepped inside. As the woman started to apologize for arriving early, Sherman knelt down and tickled the little girl. The child giggled and Sherman grinned. Sherman told Brady that he and his staff would wait for Blair. He then turned to the little girl. For nearly an hour, while his astonished generals watched, Sherman rolled around on the floor with the little girl, made grotesque faces, walked on his haunches and gave her pony rides on his back.[33]

Still waiting, Brady photographed Sherman and his staff without Blair. When Blair arrived, Brady photographed the men again. The smile Sherman displayed to the little girl faded when he faced the lens. He glared into it, and his tousled red hair and stare give him the look of an angry fighting cock.[34]

Meanwhile, tension mounted on the streets and in the camps each day as Sherman's army encountered the soldiers of the East. Sherman's soldiers were seen daring anyone to utter a negative word about Uncle Billy.[35]

"They had better look a little out or they will have General Sherman's Army to reckon with the first thing they know," an Indiana soldier said. "We don't propose to have our General called such names. Sherman a Traitor! The idea!" [36]

An Iowa private shared the outrage. "Sherman's army are with him to a man and his reputation is their reputation," he wrote.[37]

The two armies that had fought for the Union taunted each other. They continued the name-calling and fistfights broke out. As some of Sherman's Western officers drank with officers from the East, Cump's men sang "three groans to the Secretary of War," which caused more fighting.[38]

*LIA*

Brig. Gen. Joshua L. Chamberlain

"A spirit of rivalry, with a touch of dislike, existed between the West and the Army of the Potomac, which served only in the East," one Western soldier said. "They always went into winter quarters at the coming-on of winter. We campaigned right along, summer and winter, rain or shine. They did more fighting than we did, but compared with our work, theirs was like taking all day to work in half a bushel." [39]

Sherman's men were a curiosity to many civilians. The march to the sea and its devastation were well-known, but many citizens were anxious to see the soldiers. They particularly wanted to meet and talk to the bummers. This fascination with the army of Westerners did not sit well with the Eastern soldiers.[40]

A private in Sherman's army, Robert Hale Strong, wrote that Meade's men called Sherman's boys "water fowl," "Sherman's mules" and "thieves." Sherman's men retaliated, calling the Easterners "white collars," "soft breads," "white gloves" and "feather beds." [41]

When Sherman's soldiers received orders to apply for new uniforms to wear at the Grand Review, most objected because they did not want to pay for a new outfit just before heading home.[42] Some of the soldiers eventually relented, but at the last moment, many refused to wear the new uniforms and simply packed them away.[43]

Not every soldier was eager to march in the Grand Review. James Nichol, of the Army of the Potomac, wrote his wife in Pennsylvania that he was weak from diarrhea.

"I must tell you that we have a grand reveve (review) in Washington today but I did not go along for I did not feel like walking there and back again. I thout it no use to walk if I could stay in camp for it is again to be very hot today. I just thaut that I had march anuff for them." [44]

In the camp of the Army of the Potomac, the soldiers in the 5th Corps held a moving ceremony for their commander, Maj. Gen. Charles Griffin, on the eve of the Grand Review. Brig. Gen. Joshua Lawrence Chamberlain, called the savior of Gettysburg and the officer Grant picked to receive the surrender of Lee's troops at Appomattox, presented Griffin with a miniature version of the corps' battle flag, a Red Maltese cross studded with diamonds.

"First the low ripple of handclapping after common custom, but more were clasping each other's hands in emotion they knew not how to express," Chamberlain said about the ceremony. "Strong men rose to their feet or bent their heads in sobs." [45]

As record numbers of visitors continued to converge on Washington, soldiers fought and taunted one another, and workers continued to pound nails building the reviewing stands in front of the White House. This would be a grand affair.

# The President's Been Shot

## 'Now He Belongs to the Ages'

## Farewell, Mary Todd Lincoln

The sound of the hammering resounded inside the White House where a haunted Mary Todd Lincoln remained, mourning the death of her Abraham.

On April 14, 1865, as she sat next to her husband at Ford's Theatre in Washington, a "bang" interrupted the play "Our American Cousin." She saw her husband slump in his chair. The President had been shot. A man identified as John Wilkes Booth, an actor and Southern sympathizer, then jumped from the Lincolns' box onto the stage and shouted in a loud voice, "Sic semper tyrannis" ("Thus always to tyrants" — the motto of the state of Virginia). As Booth jumped, his foot became tangled in a flag that marked the Lincolns' box. He scurried away on a broken leg.[1]

*USMHI/HW*

Booth jumps from the Lincolns' box.

The President was carried across the street to a back bedroom in the William Peterson house. When Stanton learned Lincoln had been shot, he quickly arrived at the side of the dying president. "The Great Energy" immediately assumed the duties of the government. Stanton sent for Grant in Philadelphia, directed the investigation to find the guilty parties and kept the government running as Lincoln lay dying. He sent for Vice President Johnson and prepared him to take over as president. Later he would write a press release announcing the assassination.[2]

From time to time, Mrs. Lincoln would enter the room "almost insane with sudden agony, moaning and sobbing out that terrible night," recalled one general. Stanton interrupted the business of the country to console her when he had the chance.[3] The distraught Mrs. Lincoln would occasionally kiss her dying husband in an attempt to bring him back to consciousness. When that failed, she

LINCOLN'S DEATH-BED.

*USMHI*

*©Bradley Schmehl*

Mary Todd Lincoln prepares to leave the White House for the final time. Her youngest son, Tad, wearing the uniform, and her oldest son, Robert, are with her. They leave before the Grand Review.

insisted that Tad, the President's youngest son, be summoned.[4]

Shrieks of "Is he dead? Oh, is he dead?" filled the room as Mrs. Lincoln wailed.[5]

Between the shrieks, Mrs. Lincoln's hatred of Johnson resurfaced. She told Stanton that she believed Johnson had conspired with Booth to kill her husband.[6]

Mrs. Lincoln told Stanton there was evidence to support her claim in two letters that had been found in New York City after the 1864 presidential elections. The assassination trial would reveal that John Wilkes Booth had dropped the letters, one of which mentioned the name "Johnson" and described how that man wanted to "rid the world of the monster."[7]

Stanton listened and then sent Charles Dana, the Assistant Secretary of War, to Lincoln's office to find these letters. Dana found the two letters inside Lincoln's desk in an envelope marked "Assassination."[8]

©Bradley Schmehl

Elizabeth Keckley

Through the night, Stanton acted as President, Secretary of War, Secretary of State, commander-in-chief and Mrs. Lincoln's comforter. Congress was not in session, and as almost no one noticed, Stanton became a dictator.[9]

"I was profoundly impressed with Secretary Stanton's bearing all through that eventful night," said Col. A.F. Rockwell, who was at the Peterson house. "While evidently swayed by the great shock which held us all under its paralyzing influence, he was not only master of himself but unmistakably the dominating power over all. Indeed, the members of the cabinet, much as children might to their father, instinctively deferred to him in all things."[10]

In the last 20 minutes before Lincoln's death, the people in the crowded back room remained quiet. Stanton stood motionless, leaning his chin upon his left hand, his right hand holding his hat and supporting his left elbow, tears falling continually.

At 7:22 a.m. on April 15, 1865, President Lincoln died. Stanton interrupted the silence when he asked the Rev. Gurley to offer a prayer. Robert Lincoln, the President's oldest son, sobbed aloud. After the prayer, Stanton made a gesture that caught the attention of some of the men in the room:

**NORTH.**

Admit the Bearer to the

EXECUTIVE MANSION,

On WEDNESDAY, the

19th of April, 1865.

USMHI/MOLLUS

A ticket for Lincoln's funeral in the White House.

"Mr. Stanton slowly and with apparent deliberation straightened out his right arm, placed his hat for an instant on his head and then as deliberately returned it to its original position," Rockwell recalled.

As the sheet was pulled over Lincoln's face, Stanton drew the window shades and solemnly said, "He now belongs to the ages."[11]

After the President's death, Stanton offered a $50,000 reward for Booth's capture and an additional $25,000 for John Surratt and David Herold, who had stabbed Secretary of State William H. Seward. The new President, Johnson, placed a $100,000

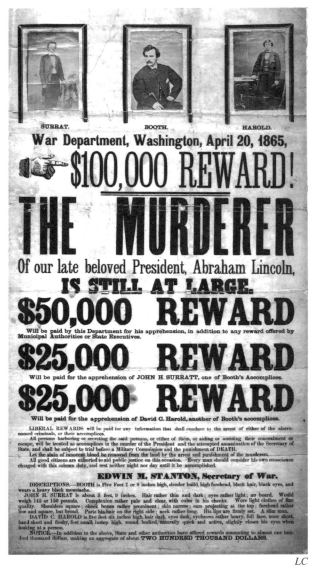

*LC*

A reward poster

reward on Confederate President Davis' head.

Booth would be killed April 26 in a Virginia barn. Conspirators Lewis Paine (or Payne or Powell or Wood as he called himself at times), Herold, Mary Surratt and George Atzerodt, who failed to assassinate Vice President Andrew Johnson, were eventually arrested and tried. They were hanged on July 7, 1865. Michael O'Laughlin, Samuel Arnold and Dr. Samuel Mudd, who had treated Booth's broken leg, were sentenced to life in prison. Edmund Spangler received six years in prison and John Surratt escaped to Canada.

The sound of Booth's derringer had propelled Mrs. Lincoln into a continued state of mourning. Her ambition centered on the White House, and now it was gone.

On Easter Sunday 1865, workers were building the wooden catafalque to hold Lincoln's coffin in the East Room. Many times when a hammer hit its mark, the sound reminded Mrs. Lincoln of the gunshot that had killed her husband.[12] Her personal seamstress, Elizabeth Keckley, described Mrs. Lincoln's mood in the bedroom in one of the first tell-all books about a public figure.

"Robert was bending over his mother with tender affection, and little Tad was crouched at the foot of the bed with a world of agony in his young face. I shall never forget the scene — the wails of a broken heart, the unearthly shrieks, the terrible convulsions, the wild, tempestuous outbursts of grief." [13]

For weeks, newspapers had speculated on when Mrs. Lincoln would leave the White House. President Johnson patiently waited as he worked from a small room in the Treasury building.

About five weeks after the assassination, Mrs. Lincoln, her two sons, her seamstress and a couple of close friends walked down the steps of the White House for the last time, on May 22, 1865, the day before the Grand Review. Mrs. Lincoln left the city she had adopted as her rightful destiny.[14]

Elizabeth Keckley described the moment.

"Now, the wife of the President was leaving the White House, and there was scarcely a friend to tell her good-by. She passed down the public stairway, entered her carriage and quietly drove to the depot. ... The silence was almost painful." [15]

# Day One of the Grand Review

## 'Get Out of the Way, You Fool!'

## Tempers Flare in the Camps

The night before the Grand Review, workers cleaned Pennsylvania Avenue. At daylight, city fire companies sprayed water onto the streets. Reveille was played in military camps, and soldiers from the Army of the Potomac prepared to move toward Pennsylvania Avenue. At 4 a.m., the 5th Corps began its march over Long Bridge, passed Maryland Avenue and stopped near First Street. By 6 a.m., the soldiers had eaten breakfast. Then the 9th Corps began to form on the street east of the Capitol, maneuvering until the head of the column reached Third Street.[1]

Civilians, dressed in their Sunday best, arrived to claim spots along Pennsylvania Avenue from the Capitol to the Executive Mansion. Later arrivals took spots behind the first row of spectators. Soon nearly every sidewalk, window, porch, balcony and rooftop was filled. The U.S. flag fluttered from nearly every house and store.[2]

For the first time since Lincoln's assassination, the flag atop the White House was not at half-mast.[3]

Hours before the event, about 2,500 public school students accompanied by teachers marched to the Capitol. The girls stopped on the steps while the boys stood on the hillside. There, they would sing "When Johnny Comes Marching Home," "Victory at Last" and "The Battle Cry of Freedom" as the soldiers marched past.[4]

*USMHI/MOLLUS*

The crowd gathers to witness the event.

Banners were hoisted along the parade route. Hung over the east portico of the Capitol was one that read, "The public schools of Washington welcome the heroes of the republic." Over the west portico stretched a banner that expressed the sentiment of a grateful nation. "The only national debt we never can pay is the debt we owe to the victorious Union soldiers." [5]

Above the entrance to the Treasury Department hung the flag of the Treasury Guard Regiment. The lower portion had been torn, not in battle, but by Booth's spur when he jumped from the President's box at Ford's Theater.[6]

Flowers adorned the main reviewing stand along with U.S. flags and banners immortalizing epic battles: "Atlanta," "Wilderness," "Stone River," "South Mountain," "Shiloh," "Vicksburg," "Gettysburg," "Savannah," "Richmond," "Petersburg" and "Cold Harbor."

Smaller stands erected by state agencies displayed the sentiments of Northern states: "Connecticut greets all who bravely fought, and weeps for all

Washington students welcome home the troops.

who fell," "Massachusetts greets the Country's Defenders," "Ohio welcomes her brave sons, and mourns for those who have fallen."[7]

The extravaganza was not without entrepreneurs appealing to the citizenry's desire for a good view of the heroes. At 15th Street, the opportunists erected a stand and charged a dollar a seat, the *Washington Evening Star* reported. Window locations sold at a premium, too, and people paid as much as $10 an hour or $50 a day for prime locations, according to the *New York Tribune*.

About an hour before the march, cavalry patrols took up positions at intersections to prevent carriages from crossing and spectators from blocking the avenue. Shortly before 9 o'clock, the stands in front of the White House filled slowly with military officers and politicians, their wives and families. Cheers from an admiring public greeted them.[8]

Photographers Alexander Gardner of Washington and Brady of New York began setting up their equipment to capture the grand pageant.[9]

At exactly 9 a.m., the report of a gun shattered the drone of the crowd and announced the beginning of the Grand Review. Under a blazing sun, the grand marshal rode slowly down the avenue. Behind him marched a color guard with massed flags. A solitary horseman in a major's uniform followed, riding a handsome steed, and newspaper reporters strained to identify the soldier. It was "Old Snapping Turtle," Maj. Gen. George G. Meade, riding his show horse, Blackie, a few paces in front of his staff as commander of the Army of the Potomac.

As Meade rode along the avenue, Pennsylvanians rose and cheered, and someone shouted "Gettysburg!"[10]

Meade's military position, like that of many others, had been ordained by the late President. Lincoln had tapped Meade to be commander of the Army of the Potomac on June 28,

©*Bradley Schmehl*

Maj. Gen. George G. Meade

43

The crowd watches as troops pass in review.

HW

Meade passes in review.

1863, a couple of days before the Battle of Gettysburg. A surprised Meade hesitated but accepted the honor.[11] Though he won the fight at Gettysburg, Meade lost the respect of Lincoln when he allowed Lee to escape back to Virginia. Meade offered his resignation, but it was refused.[12]

Approaching the reviewing stand, Meade turned in his saddle to face the dignitaries. He drew his sword and raised the blade to the sun, saluting the most important chairs in the reviewing stand. But they were empty. From across the street, the crowd chanted "Gettysburg, Gettysburg."[13]

Meade passed the reviewing stand around 9:30 a.m., got off Blackie and walked up the steps onto Stand No. 1. As Meade's soldiers marched by, a carriage dashed up the street and stopped in front of the main reviewing stand. The crowd let out a great cheer as President Johnson and Stanton emerged and took two of the empty seats on Stand No. 1.[14] Soon, Welles and other cabinet members arrived. Grant walked onto the stand a short time later with his staff and two young sons. Sherman also arrived.[15]

Meade and some of his generals had passed the main reviewing stand without having the honor of being reviewed.

It might have seemed Grant had publicly snubbed Meade. Military officials knew Grant did not think highly of the commander of the Army of the Potomac.[16] But Grant was too aware of public opinion to affront Meade, especially on this occasion. Grant was tied up on government business related to E. Kirby Smith's Trans-Mississippi Confederate troops that were still active in Texas, and Napoleon III's placement of Maximillian of Austria as a puppet dictator in Mexico.[17]

Grant had ordered Gen. Philip H. Sheridan, the hero of the Shenandoah Valley campaign, to the West on May 17, 1865, to

# The Main Reviewing Stand

President Johnson is in the center. To his right are Stanton and Grant.

President Andrew Johnson

A division of artillery passes in review.

deal with both issues. Sheridan, however, did not want to leave Washington until after the Grand Review, "for naturally I had a strong desire to head my command on that great occasion," he said in his memoirs.[18]

On the main reviewing stand, the dignitaries were finally in place. In the center sat President Johnson, the self-educated blacksmith from Tennessee whom the Republican Party tapped as Lincoln's running mate in 1864 when Johnson stood as the only U.S. senator from a Southern state to support the Union. The seat to his right was reserved for each commander of a corps as it was being reviewed. Next were seats for Stanton, Grant and Attorney General Speed. The seats to the left of Johnson were occupied by Postmaster-General William Dennison, Secretary of the Navy Welles, Sherman, Meade and Quartermaster General Montgomery Megis. Other civil and military officials filled the rest of the stand.[19]

Stanton, despite his problems with Sherman, enjoyed the day. As the soldiers marched by, he recounted to those around him the stories behind the battles, the losses, victories and the personalities of the war.[20]

"You see in these armies, the foundation of the Republic — our future railway managers, congressmen, bank presidents, senators, manufacturers, judges, governors and diplomats; yes and not less than half a dozen presidents," Stanton exclaimed.[21]

Behind Meade and his staff marched the nearly 80,000 soldiers of the Army of the Potomac who had survived punishing battles in the last four years. At times, they had been the victims of poor leadership and witnessed comrades being sacrificed on bloody battlefields.

Here marched the men who had learned about war at the first Bull Run, where they were nearly crushed by the enemy only to rise again. They had withstood the hell of the seven-day battle in the Peninsula, snatched victory from their worthy foe at Antietam. These were the survivors of the bloody affairs at Chancellorsville and Fredericksburg, the soldiers who fought at Gettysburg on Little Round

Top and in Devil's Den. These were the defenders of the nation's capital and the men who charged at Petersburg and saw Lee finally bow to their pressure at Appomattox.[22]

After Meade passed in review, Sheridan's cavalry, now under the command of Wesley Merritt, followed. The clattering of horses' hooves continued for more than an hour as the cavalry passed.[23]

The crowd, swollen with anticipation, recognized one of the next war heroes nearing the stands. Young ladies pushed forward and older women gawked when Maj. Gen. George Armstrong Custer appeared. At age 26, he was the youngest general in the Union Army and a veteran of virtually every important battle with the Army of the Potomac. The commander had attained legendary status.

Dressed in his unorthodox attire, with blond hair falling to his shoulders and a generous mustache and goatee, Custer was the star of the Grand Review's first day.[24]

As Custer rode at the head of his division, a woman tossed him a wreath of flowers for his already decorated horse, a powerful steed he called Don Juan. This spooked the horse, some observers said. The horse bolted, and Custer struggled to stay in the saddle as the animal ran partially sideways from the east side of the White House to the west gate. With his red necktie flying and his hat and saber on the ground, Custer passed the reviewing stand while trying to control the horse. Even during the pandemonium, Custer had the presence of mind to bow to the dignitaries as the crowd chanted his name, "Custer! Custer!"[25]

A mounted guard rode into the street in front of Custer's horse in an attempt to bring the steed under control. Custer

*USMHI/MOLLUS*

Troops pass in review.

*USMHI*

Maj. Gen. George Custer riding his steed.

47

Mounted troops file down Pennsylvania Avenue.

Troops march down Pennsylvania Avenue.

yelled to the man, "Get out of the way, you fool! Get out of the way!" [26] Custer turned Don Juan around and rode swiftly back, saluting the President again, and resumed his position at the front of his division as it was being reviewed.[27]

Thus, Custer was the only soldier to be reviewed twice.

Behind Custer marched his division, men who had taken on the look of their flamboyant commander. Each man had a red scarf or tie, known as the "Custer Tie," thrown back over his shoulders. The ties were made of every material imaginable from the finest silk to the coarsest flannel.

Other troops that brought color to the pageantry were the Zouaves, volunteer regiments wearing blue attire trimmed with red and complete with crimson skull caps with blue tassels.[28]

Next came the mounted artillery of the regular army. Their gleaming polished cannons symbolized America's military strength. The Provost Marshal's Brigade that followed highlighted the army's engineering brilliance. The pioneers hauled pontoons, used to erect portable bridges, and other equipment rarely seen in a holiday military show.[29]

An engineering brigade officer unintentionally provided laughter for some of the people on the main reviewing stand. The officer wore a modified French chasseur cap, which was not regulation headgear. The cap included an extra measure of cloth between the lower band and the crown. As he saluted the President, the officer bowed his head. At the same time, his horse kicked up and put down its head. The unexpected display from the animal sent the officer's head even lower, and the crown of his cap fell forward, "letting out the superfluous cloth till it looked like an accordion extended at full length."

"The sight was so ludicrous that several of us who were standing just behind the

Aerial view of the troops marching in the Grand Review.

President burst out into a poorly suppressed laugh," said Gen. Horace Porter. "This moved him (the officer) to turn squarely round and glare at us savagely." [30]

Next arrived Meade's infantry. These soldiers displayed parade-ground precision. From the Capitol past the reviewing stand up to 17th Street, the troops marched in a quick-time cadence, left-right-left-right-left, the soldiers' feet hitting the dirt street in unison, their arms carried at right shoulder. Behind each brigade of infantry were six mule-drawn ambulances three abreast. The rear of the corps was brought up by a brigade of artillery.

When the troops approached the reviewing stand, only the mounted officers saluted the dignitaries. The marching soldiers maintained their cadence until they had passed in review. The Easterners cut a dashing swath down Pennsylvania Avenue. [31]

To keep the troops fresh, the city's Sanitary Commission employed about 100 men to hand out ice water to any thirsty soldier.

Nothing touched the hearts of the spectators so deeply as the sight of soldiers carrying old war flags. These precious bullet-riddled, battle-stained war remnants brought tears to some eyes, and many people broke through guards and rushed into the street just to press their lips to the fabric. [32]

In front of the Treasury Department, the crowds made it difficult for the soldiers to pass. Along the line of guards stationed in front of the State Department to keep back the throngs, the pressure at times was so great that life and limb were jeopardized, the *Washington Evening Star* reported.

The 2nd Brigade of the 2nd Division of the 5th Corps felt the pressure of the crowd. When the brigade reached Seventh Street, a large number of Marylanders rushed into the street and greeted the men with three hearty cheers and continued to cheer until the entire corps had passed, the *Washington Evening Star* reported.

Missing from the crowds were some of Sherman's soldiers who refused to witness the review of the Easterners. The bad blood between the two armies would resurface that night. [33]

Those Westerners who were present witnessed a scene to remember. The Eastern soldiers sported new uniforms, and their shoes and belts were polished.

"Their buckles and eagles (insignia) were bright as stars. They all wore white gloves and white

*USMHI/FL*

The Grand Review from the Treasury building.

collars. They marched with a short step, in perfect time, every foot moving in unison with comrades' feet. They were a splendid set of men, and were cheered by us and by the spectators," said Robert Hale Strong, a private from Sherman's army.[34]

Column after column of soldiers passed the reviewing stand.

"It is or was then, part of military drill that when the order to halt came on review or parade, every gun must come to 'right shoulder arms' in perfect time, none too slow, none too soon. Each regiment on review came to 'shoulder' perfectly. It was a sight to watch," one soldier wrote.[35]

As music floated down the thoroughfare, accused assassination conspirators Arnold and Mudd rose from their seats to look out the courtroom window, the *Washington Evening*

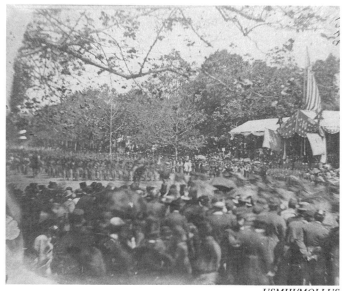

*USMHI/MOLLUS*

The troops cut a dashing swath near the main reviewing stand.

*Star* reported. The judge assigned to the trial decided to postpone testimony after it was learned that witnesses could not get across Pennsylvania Avenue. He ruled the trial would continue the day after the last troops were reviewed. (Later, it should be recognized, the government said the trial was suspended to allow time for the examination of 8 tons of Confederate documents forwarded to the War Department by "Old Joe," Confederate Gen. Joseph E. Johnston, the man whom Jefferson F. Davis removed from command at Atlanta.[36])

Meanwhile, at Fort Monroe, Virginia, Davis and some of his Confederate cabinet members were led from a steamer to prison cells. No one was allowed to approach within 500 yards. "Old Brains" Halleck was in charge.[37]

Back in Washington, on the reviewing stand, Sherman spoke constantly with his brother, John the senator, and Cump's father-in-law. Sherman commented on how Meade's men marched and noted how some sneaked a peak at the people on the reviewing stand. They "turned their eyes around like country gawks to look at the big people on the stand," he said. He also observed the marching was poor probably because of music provided by two civilian orchestras "taught to play the very latest operas." Sherman decided his troops would not make the same mistake. They would march to their own regimental bands.[38]

At one point, Sherman turned to Meade and said, "I'm afraid my poor tadder-demalion corps will make a poor appearance tomorrow when contrasted with yours." Meade, no fan of Sherman, assured him that the public would understand.[39]

President Johnson remained busy doffing his hat as the crowd cheered. The way Johnson handled his hat caught the attention of many of the spectators. He would hold it by the brim with his right hand, and waving it from left to right, occasionally rest the hat on his left shoulder.

After the 9th Corps had passed in review and before the arrival of the 5th Corps, spectators rushed the reviewing stand and called the name of President Johnson. He rose, bowed to the throng and sat down. Then the throng called for Grant, who also rose to acknowledge the cheers.[40]

Spectators then called Sherman's name, but according to the *Chicago Tribune,* the general had left the stand. The *Washington Daily Chronicle*

*HW*

Davis in his cell at Fort Monroe.

*USMHI/MOLLUS*

The crowd moves toward the main reviewing stand.

Two women cross Pennsylvania Avenue as mounted troops pass in review.

A soldier stops to pose for the camera.

also reported that Sherman had left the stand and was seen "shaking hands with some old friends" on Stand No. 4 and "conversing in his quick, nervous manner, his face beaming with delight."

The *New York World,* however, reported something different. The paper wrote that when the crowd called Sherman's name "and while the whole mass is waiting for the gallant leader to rise and reply, who should stand up but Secretary Stanton, and bow in the most conciliatory manner. Sherman kept his seat, content with the plaudits and too great to claim them."

The 5th Corps finally arrived at the main reviewing stand. The President and his cabinet and the dignitaries stood and cheered. This was the corps that had accepted Lee's surrender at Appomattox.

Griffin and his commanders saluted the President and Grant. They dismounted and walked up the steps of the main stand and sat next to the President to review their corps. As Chamberlain sat watching from the reviewing stand, he could hear the murmuring of the crowd, "This is the 5th Corps," "These are straight from Five Forks and Appomattox." [41]

After the 5th Corps passed in review, the 2nd Corps marched toward the reviewing stand. This was the last corps of the Army of the Potomac to be reviewed. And what an ending to the first day! The famed Irish Brigade marched in perfect step with every soldier and officer wearing a sprig of pine in his hat that bore the regimental emblem, emerald-green grounds with a sunburst and the harp of Erin. The men wearing these colors were cheered up and down Pennsylvania Avenue. [42] The 2nd Corps commander, Maj. Gen. A. A. Humphreys, and his staff rode down the avenue on white horses. The *Washington Daily Chronicle* wrote that Humphreys' staff chose white horses to honor their commander, who always rode a white or gray horse. "In the hottest of the fight, General Humphreys could always be discovered, at night as well as day, on his favorite white steed, the same that he rode yesterday," the paper reported.

At Willard's Hotel, Pennsylvania Gov. Andrew Curtin had several state flags placed in the windows. The soldiers from Pennsylvania cheered the flags and Curtin, who stood at a window. Curtin bowed to acknowledge the cheers.[43]

After six hours, the last of Meade's soldiers had passed the reviewing stand. In all, 29 regiments of cavalry, 33 batteries of artillery and 180 infantry units had passed in review along with numerous division and corps commanders.[44]

The 6th Corps was not reviewed the first day because the soldiers had remained in Virginia. This corps had its own review on June 8, 1865.

Newspapers noted that no colored troops participated in the first day's procession. The black soldiers had been organized and were being sent to Sheridan's new command in the Southwest.[45]

The *Daily Illinois State Journal* and other newspapers voiced outrage about the slight of the colored troops in a May 24 story.

"If (Negro troops) were in the vicinity and were intentionally excluded from the display, the fact should cause a feeling of shame to tingle upon the cheek of every loyal man in the land," the newspaper editorialized. "The troops, who have met the common foe and assisted to vanquish him, had a right to be represented here as they were upon the field of battle."

*USMHI/MOLLUS*

This appears to be Maj. Gen. A.A. Humphreys and staff passing in review. Note the white horses.

*USMHI/MOLLUS*

Mounted troops and the crowd near the main reviewing stand.

President Johnson turning to leave was the signal for the spectators in the stands to rise. The crowd near the reviewing stands then rushed the main platform, blocking the path of the dignitaries to their carriages. The President's way was cleared by his secretaries, but Grant had a greater problem. The crowd swelled around him and "pushed him hither and thither in a most unseemly way." One spectator described the moment. "Sure we've seen all the sojers, and now we want to see the big sojer of all." [46]

Around 5:15 that evening, some of the revelers were treated to the sight of Grant, accompanied only by an orderly, riding his horse down Pennsylvania Avenue. Cheers arose from the onlookers and Grant acknowledged the crowds with a tip of his hat.[47]

Though some people began leaving Washington, many others were arriving. The next day, the Army of the Tennessee and the Army of Georgia would occupy Pennsylvania Avenue.

The event kept Washington police busy. During the first day, police arrested and then sent away on the evening train a number of people who walked through the crowd picking pockets. Some 15 other "equally suspicious" people were placed in jail until after the Grand Review "when they will be sent to their proper homes — Philadelphia, New York, etc.," the *Washington Evening Star* reported.

Police also closed nearly 20 restaurants and saloons that had violated orders by selling alcohol. Guards were posted at these establishments. A gift-store owner was fined $50 for swindling soldiers. A couple of soldiers caught stealing and causing other problems were arrested, and a man and a woman were injured when they were struck by an ambulance.[48]

Later in the evening, the rivalry between the two Union armies intensified. One Eastern soldier said some members of Sherman's army were bullies and "threatened to come over and burst us up" and "clean us out." Some of Sherman's men insulted members of the Army of the Potomac by saying, "You are babies and hospital cats" and "We had to send Grant and Sheridan up to teach you how to fight" and "You wouldn't have caught him (Lee) if we hadn't marched two thousand miles to drive him into the trap." The insults enraged some of the Eastern soldiers.

"But we had some 'Bowery Boys' and Fire Zouaves in our army too," Chamberlain said, "and what they wanted was to get at these 'Sherman's Bummers' and settle the question in their own ... fashion." The rift between the two Union armies became so great that Eastern division commanders had to seriously consider a line of defense.

"We doubled all camp guards, and detailed special reserves ready for a rush," Chamberlain said, "sleeping ourselves some nights in boots, with sword and pistol by our sides. This was a serious condition of things. No wonder Sherman asked to move his army to the other side of the river."[49]

Grant was informed about the problems and eventually intervened. He suggested to Sherman that he post guards around his camps and prohibit soldiers from leaving. Grant did not want the public to see this rift between the two Union armies.

"What we want is to preserve quiet and decorum and without apparently making any distinction between the different Armies," Grant said.[50]

But Grant's intervention came too late. According to a *New York Tribune* correspondent, some of Sherman's soldiers and members of the 5th Corps clashed in Virginia, resulting in several deaths and numerous injuries.[51]

While most officials rested after an emotional day, the Army of the Tennessee began to march from its campsite in the rear of Arlington Heights to the Long Bridge on the Virginia side of the Potomac. This army would be the first to appear on Pennsylvania Avenue during the second day of the parade.[52]

# Day Two of the Grand Review
## The Look of a Proud Conqueror
## The Greatest Event in History

GRAND REVIEW AT WASHINGTON—SHERMAN'S VETERANS CROSSING LONG BRIDGE, MAY 24, 1865.—[PHOTOGRAPHED BY A. GARDNER, WASHINGTON, D. C.]

*HW*

Morning newspapers of May 24 filled their pages with stories about the glorious first day of the review. The accounts described the dignitaries on the main reviewing stand, the crowds that poured into Washington, the order in which troops marched and how President Johnson and members of his cabinet arrived late. Reporters explained, in different ways, what led Custer's steed, Don Juan, to dash past the main reviewing stand. The *New York Tribune* reported that Custer would miss the second day of the review because he was sent West to join Sheridan. The *Daily Illinois State Journal* reported that the 8 tons of Confederate documents forwarded to the War Department by Gen. Joseph E. Johnston arrived in 83 boxes that filled six wagons.

A 10-word front page news brief also reported that Secretary of State Seward, healing from the assassination attempt, was expected to be on the reviewing stand. Readers also were fascinated by a newspaper report that said Sherman had written a letter for publication in which he "abuses the War Department and quotes Shakespeare to a considerable extent." [1] The *New York Tribune* threw fuel on the Stanton-Sherman fire when it reported that Sherman's officers were urging the removal of Stanton from office and that "a demonstration of displeasure is looked for from the rank and file when they pass the official stand" at the Grand Review.[2]

The city was in a festive mood, but Sherman remained bitter.

At his campsite, Sherman reminded his soldiers "all eyes forward" and no "gawking" when they neared the reviewing stand.[3]

Before daylight, city fire crews again sprayed water on the streets. At dawn, the Army of the Tennessee moved across the Long Bridge and up to Maryland Avenue to the north and east of the Capitol.[4]

The morning air was chilly, but the sun eventually warmed the day. Crowds again lined the streets and all the banners and mottoes remained in place. Police moved to block the intersections.[5]

Shortly before 9 o'clock, a carriage drove up to the reviewing stand and Secretary of War Stanton and President Johnson emerged. As Johnson took his seat, the crowd greeted him with cheers. Many of the same dignitaries and their families that had been present the day before filled the stands again today. Ellen Sherman and Julia Grant sat next to each other with Margaretta Meade nearby.[6]

This day, the crowd near the main reviewing stand was much larger.

Stand No. 4 began filling with soldiers from hospitals. Wounded veterans also filled Stand No. 3, where deaf students from the famous school under the charge of Edward Miner Gallaudet were assembling.[7]

*LC*

Secretary of State William H. Seward

*USMHI/MOLLUS*

The crowd at one of the reviewing stands.

Oliver O. Howard

*LC*

Sherman and his two armies had gathered at the beginning of the parade route. Gen. Oliver O. Howard was at his side. Sherman had asked Howard to ride next to him and not, as would be expected, as the commander of the Army of the Tennessee. Howard had been named on May 12, 1865, commissioner of the Freedman's Bureau, the government agency that oversaw the transition of slaves to freedmen. Howard wanted to ride at the head of his old command, but Sherman appealed to him to defer to "Black Jack" Logan, who had been named commander of the Army of the Tennessee the previous day.[8] Howard objected, but Sherman reasoned with him.

"Howard, you are a Christian, and won't mind such a sacrifice," Sherman told him. Howard answered, "Surely, if you put it on that ground, I submit."[9]

As the church bells chimed at 9 o'clock, Lt. Col. W. H. Ross, chief of artillery of the 15th Corps, fired the signal gun to start the final day of the Grand Review. Howard again pleaded with Sherman to allow him to ride at the head of the Army of the Tennessee.

Sherman replied, "No. Howard, you shall ride with me."

Sherman and his staff wheeled into line on Pennsylvania Avenue. As they proceeded, a band played "The Battle Hymn of the Republic," a version of the song soldiers sang as they left a ruined Atlanta in 1864. The avenue was so densely packed that the troops found it almost impossible to maneuver. As Sherman rode down the avenue, Howard reined back his horse in an attempt to allow Sherman to lead and to receive the glory due him. Sherman motioned to Howard and then insisted the one-armed general ride by his side. Howard pulled his horse next to Sherman's.[10]

Behind Sherman waited his 65,000 soldiers, including the bummers and some of the freedmen who had followed him to Washington. The Army of the Tennessee was composed of 94 regiments of infantry while the Army of Georgia had 86 regiments and a full complement of artillery as well as a contingent of cavalry.[11]

"If yesterday was one of the grandest military pageants ever witnessed on this continent, today carried off the palm of being the grandest ever known in the history of modern times. The interest to see this review was far greater than the day before," the *Cincinnati Commercial* reported.

In front of Sherman, almost like bodyguards, rode the 9th Illinois Mounted Infantry. The soldiers attempted to clear the street before Sherman and Howard passed, but the throngs would not be denied. They pressed up to Sherman, presenting him with gifts and wreaths.[12]

Crowds of women on balconies begged Sherman to look toward them, but his head

*LC*

The crowd near the Treasury building.

remained straight. Some thought Sherman was unmoved by the cheers, but he was just following his own orders — "hold eyes front." [13]

At one point, Sherman was presented with two large wreaths of flowers. One was placed around the neck of Lexington, Sherman's Kentucky thoroughbred; the other was hung from his shoulder. Howard and his horse also were decorated. [14]

His soldiers hardly recognized Uncle Billy. His hair was cut and he was wearing a new uniform. Throughout the war, Sherman had dressed no better than his men. [15]

A view of the crowd at the Treasury building.

Arriving in front of Maj. Gen. Christopher Augur's headquarters, Sherman broke his steely demeanor. He removed his hat, rode close to the building and bowed low to someone in a second-story window. The crowd near the building looked around to see who was receiving this honor. It was Secretary of State Seward, who never made it to the main reviewing stand, as the newspapers predicted. [16]

As Sherman neared the Treasury building, he was tempted to turn around to see his soldiers. But he resisted. He disliked this type of pageantry and likely remembered the fiasco in Goldsboro, North Carolina, when he had stopped a review of his motley troops in front of newly arrived officers. More than half of his men had been barefoot. They wore torn trousers and showed bare legs. The soldiers sported all kinds of headgear, from beaver skins to bandannas. He had wanted to proudly display his soldiers, but they laughed and cursed as they marched. One guest called the affair "a sorry sight."

Sherman was forced to apologize to his guests. They "don't march very well, but they will fight," he explained. [17]

In Washington, he did not want to be embarrassed by his troops.

Sherman had emphasized "all eyes forward," but now he was ready to violate his own order. He turned in his saddle and looked at his troops. Here marched the same soldiers who embarrassed him in Goldsboro. But today they showed Uncle Billy their best side. "The sight was simply magnificent," Sherman recalled. "The column was compact and the glittering muskets looked like a solid mass of steel moving with the regularity of a pendulum. It was the happiest and most satisfactory moment in my life." [18]

Sherman swung front again, and one observer wrote that in the 45-year-old

When Sherman turned around, he saw his soldiers in tight formation.

general's eyes was "the proud, conscious glare of the conqueror."

Farther along the route, a veteran reserve soldier approached Sherman with another bouquet. Sherman's horse became jumpy, and he motioned the soldier back. "Give it to Howard!" the people shouted, but Howard could not take it because he had only one arm. The veteran returned to his seat with the bouquet amid the cheers of the crowd.[19]

Near the main reviewing stand, a deafening cheer announced the approach of the conquering hero. The band began playing the song he had made famous, "Marching Through Georgia." Sherman "came up with the light of battle on his face," one newspaper noted. Another newspaper, the *Philadelphia Evening Bulletin*, reported the cheering nearly drowned out the music of the band.

Sherman remained focused, his eyes fixed upon President Johnson and

*FL*

Sherman and Howard pass in review.

Grant. As he rode by the reviewing stand, he saluted the President with his sword. At his side, Howard placed the reins of his horse in his mouth, drew his sword with his left hand and saluted. The two men then dismounted and ascended the steps of the platform.[20]

Noah Brooks, the famed newspaper correspondent, watched from a stand across the street. He was seated between a senator from California and one from Massachusetts. When Sherman emerged on the platform, the Senator from Massachusetts excitedly said to Brooks, "Now let us watch Sherman; people think he will affront Stanton, whom he hasn't met yet."

The pair focused their field glasses and watched.[21]

Sherman knew all eyes were upon him, and that his soldiers in spite of their commander's wishes were stealing a glance as well.

Sherman shook hands with his father-in-law and embraced his son, Tom. He was then met with more handshaking. Those sitting on the reviewing stand were tense, for all knew Sherman had not reconciled with Stanton and the inevitable was seconds away.

"In a group of notable men on the grandstand, Sherman was certainly the most notable in appearance," Brooks wrote. "His head was high and narrow, his hair and whiskers were sandy in hue, his moustache stiff and bristling, and his eyes keen and piercing. He was very tall, walked with an immense stride, talked rapidly and nervously, and would be picked out in any assemblage as a man of distinction. All eyes were fastened upon his striking countenance, the vast multitude gazing with a certain rapture at the famous man whom they now saw for the first time." [22]

Finally, Sherman reached President Johnson and shook his hand. Between the President and Grant sat Stanton. Grant, like everyone else, was tense about the situation since Sherman had refused his request that he reconcile with Stanton.[23]

Sherman moved toward Stanton. This was the man who had embarrassed him in Savannah when Stanton told him to arrange the meeting with the 20 black men; the man who accused Sherman of seeking the presidency; the man who approved Halleck's order for Sherman's officers to disobey him; the man who let loose the press against Sherman after the Johnston surrender; the man who refused to apologize after implying Sherman was a traitor.

Sherman already had taken his revenge against Halleck in Richmond, and now it was Stanton's turn.

Stanton slowly arose. In front of him stood the arrogant general who cut all lines of communication after leaving Atlanta and forced Northerners to learn of his march from Southern newspapers; the man who refused to obey federal law on the enlistment of black soldiers; the man who said he would not complicate matters when dealing with Confederate Joe Johnston; the man who publicly attacked the War Secretary; the man who announced when he arrived near Washington that he was "untamed and unconquered."

The crowd near the reviewing stand pushed forward, focusing on the two men. Ellen Sherman and Julia Grant watched intently, for they knew the hatred Sherman harbored toward Stanton.

Sherman's face, marked by a dark scar, was crimson. His red hair seemed to stand on end. Stanton, now erect, cautiously extended his hand. Sherman, with fire in his eyes, refused to acknowledge it and quickly moved to his "sworn friend" Grant. He shook Grant's hand, made a comment and then became absorbed into the mass of people, where he would stand for six hours watching his troops march. "Stanton's face, never very expressive, remained immobile," Brooks reported.[24]

The historic incident occurred in just seconds and was reported in many different ways. Some said Sherman had put his hands behind him and had made a remark as he attempted to upstage Stanton. Assistant Secretary of War Dana wrote that he had positioned himself behind Stanton waiting for this moment to occur. He said Stanton did not offer a hand to Sherman but "gave him merely a slight forward motion of his head." [25] A gossip columnist from Washington claimed Sherman told Stanton, "I do not care to shake hands with clerks."

In his memoirs, however, Sherman simply noted that he shook hands with the President, Grant and each member of the cabinet. "As I approached Mr. Stanton," Sherman explained, "he offered me his hand, but I declined it publicly, and the fact was universally noticed." [26]

The *Chicago Tribune* reported that

*USMHI/MOLLUS*

The crowd pushes forward toward the main reviewing stand.

after Sherman refused the hand of Stanton, the crowd noticed and "in the enthusiasm of the moment loudly applauded the act and even laughed at Stanton's discomfort."

As Sherman moved quickly away from Stanton, the Rev. Justin D. Fulton of Brooklyn, New York, said he shouted from seats left of the main grandstand in support of the Secretary of War.

"Edwin M. Stanton, savior of our country under God, rise and receive the greetings of your friends," Fulton called.[27]

Sherman's face "was black," Fulton later related. President Johnson motioned to Stanton to rise but the Secretary of War remained seated. Again Fulton called on Stanton, "Edwin M. Stanton, savior of our country under God, rise and receive the greetings of your friends."

Stanton arose, and Fulton shouted, "Nine cheers for the savior of his country under God!" The crowd cheered and Stanton "received a recognition which would not have come to him had Sherman acted the gentleman," Fulton said.[28]

Next, the Army of the Tennessee, with Logan as its commander, marched down the route. The crowd quickly began comparing these soldiers to those who marched the day before. Sherman had less artillery and very little of his cavalry while Meade's army had only part of its infantry.[29]

The Western men were taller, with fewer boys and scarcely any foreigners. Their stride was about six inches longer — more of a left-and-right-and-left-and-right-and-left — yet they stepped in unison. Their yellow and red beards and light hair were worn long. One could not distinguish officers from men, except by their uniforms. Eastern men wore the close-fitting regulation skull cap; the Western men the soft slouch hat. The Easterners were exact, prim and stiff; the Westerners easy, carefree, independent and pioneerish.[30]

One of the Westerners described the

*USMHI/MOLLUS*

Looking up Pennsylvania Avenue from the Treasury building. Maj. Gen. Logan and staff and the Army of the Tennessee pass in review.

*USMHI/MOLLUS*

The troops march in tight formation.

difference. "We moved in a sort of springy manner instead of with the stiff motion of the Eastern boys," he said. Instead of neat, well-packed knapsacks, "We wore our blanket rolls over our shoulders ... with the ends tied together to make a loop of blanket, the knotted end hanging down under our left arm. We were tanned and sunburnt. There was not a white collar or a pair of gloves among a thousand men." [31]

From the reviewing stand, Grant made this observation: The Army of the Potomac "had been operating where they received directly from the North full supplies of food and clothing regularly." They were well-drilled, he continued, well-disciplined and orderly soldiers who lacked the experience of gathering their food and supplies in an enemy's country. Sherman's army was not as well-dressed as the Army of the Potomac, "But their marching could not be excelled; they gave the appearance of men who had been thoroughly drilled to endure hardships, either by long and continuous marches or through exposure to any climate, without the ordinary shelter of a camp," Grant said. [32]

The *New York Tribune* reported that when the 15th Corps neared the reviewing stand, officers shouted something to the soldiers, and the men, without turning their heads, relaxed their stoic faces and broke into wild yells, tearing off their hats and waving them in the air — their eyes still front. [33]

As each regimental commander passed the stand, he saluted with his sword. Company officers and soldiers in perfect time brought their weapons to right shoulder.

Music filled the air as a band preceded each division, marching from the Capitol to the Treasury. Brigade musicians played patriotic songs as their units passed the reviewing officer.

After some of the soldiers passed the reviewing stand, reporters and citizens

*USMHI/MOLLUS*

Sherman's Army of Georgia, 20th Army Corps passes in review.

*USMHI/MOLLUS*

A brigade band leads mounted troops.

rushed up and asked the names of the regiments. All kind of answers were offered: "Hooker's Company," "Sherman's Bummers," "Sherman's Webfeet." [34]

"Our boys took on an appearance of glory and holiness, and they marched, oh how they marched, never before did they stride like that," a Wisconsin soldier wrote home. "I thought we would lose some more buttons for our chests swelled up and our hearts throbbed." [35]

Every officer who wore an empty sleeve or showed that he had been wounded was greeted with a cheer. Howard received the loudest tribute.[36]

Behind Logan's Army of the Tennessee marched Maj. Gen. Slocum's Army of Georgia. "They march like the lords of the world," the German ambassador noted.

When Sherman's 15th Corps passed, the German ambassador was heard to say "An army like that could whip all Europe." As the 20th Corps passed, the ambassador said, "An army like that could whip the world." And when Jefferson C. Davis' 14th Corps went by near the end of the parade, the ambassador quipped, "An army like that could whip the devil." [37]

The crowd had the opportunity to see Sherman's soldiers as they might have looked while marching through the South, though now they were more orderly. And the review of Sherman's army could not have been complete without the sight of the bummers and the freedmen.

Gen. Porter described the unique elements of Sherman's army, the troops, blacks, bummers and all.

"Each division was followed by a pioneer corps of negroes, marching in double ranks, with picks, spades, and axes slung across their brawny shoulders, their stalwart form conspicuous by their height. ... Six ambulances followed each division

SWEETS FROM THE SWEET—THE GRAND REVIEW—LADIES PRESENTING FLOWERS TO SHERMAN'S COLOR-BEARERS NEAR THE WHITE HOUSE.—
A SKETCH BY OUR SPECIAL ARTIST, J. E. TAYLOR.

*FL*

*USMHI/MOLLUS*

Bummers on parade.

*USMHI/MOLLUS*

Six ambulances follow a division.

THE GRAND REVIEW AT WASHINGTON, D. C., MAY 23—HEADQUARTERS OF GEN. AUGER—SHERMAN'S BUMMERS AND FORAGERS PASSING.—FROM A SKETCH BY OUR SPECIAL ARTIST, J. E. TAYLOR.

*FL*

Blacks who followed Sherman's army north take part in the Grand Review.

to represent its baggage-train; and then came the amusing spectacle of 'Sherman's bummers' bearing with them the spoils of war." [38]

The bummers displayed their trophies: mules loaded with turkeys, geese and chickens. Porter said that "cows, goats, sheep, donkeys, crowing roosters and in one instance a chattering monkey" followed.

Behind Blair's corps appeared probably the most incongruous sight ever in a military formation. A brigade of black servants, attended by the guards of a small baggage train, was preceded by two children riding a donkey. Some of the black men were armed with pistols and knives. Some spectators cheered these marchers while others jeered them. [39]

Led by blacks, the strangest combination of beasts streamed down Pennsylvania Avenue. Mules, asses, horses, colts, cows,

*USMHI/MOLLUS*

Wagons roll down Pennsylvania Avenue.

sheep, pigs, goats, raccoons, chickens and dogs. Every beast of burden was loaded to capacity with tents, knapsacks, hampers, containers, boxes, valises, kettles, pots, pans, dishes, bird cages, cradles, mirrors, fiddles and clothing. Children and black women rode atop many of the pack animals.[40]

As Blair's corps reached Willard's Hotel, about 150 men, mainly from Missouri, presented the general with a banner and each of the officers of his staff a bouquet, The *New York Tribune* reported.

Around 3:30 p.m., the last of Sherman's troops marched past the reviewing stand. As Sherman attempted to leave the stand, crowds pushed toward him, just as they had with Grant the previous day. Sherman tried to maintain a patient dignity, but finally he snapped, "Damn you, get out of the way! Get out of the way!" [41]

The event was over. Washington remained in a festive mood, and Sherman had his revenge.

Grant, Sherman and other military leaders, as well as politicians, called the Grand Review a great success. Newspapers cast it in a more historic light.

The *New York Times* called it "one of the most important events of a life time." Another said the Grand Review "is spoken of as the greatest which has ever taken place on this continent."

Another newspaper summed up the end of the Grand Review: "The army marched through Washington and then, as an army, disappeared forever, absorbed into the body-politic, a million men of war turned men of peace in a single day."

The Philadelphia Inquirer was the only daily newspaper to print an image of the Grand Review the day after the event.

# Part II

# The South's Lost Cause

by Dr. Charles Reagan Wilson

IN JANUARY 1866, the women of Columbus, Georgia, asked the people of their community to make plans to decorate Confederate graves. They are often credited with initiating the celebration of Confederate Memorial Day and more generally the honoring of the Confederate memory after the war. A Confederate widow asked Southerners to set apart a day "to be handed down through time as a religious custom of the South to wreathe the graves of our martyred dead with flowers." Other women across the South had the same idea, though, and many communities claim the origin of the commemoration of the Lost Cause, the South's post-Civil War memory of the Confederacy as a heroic, noble endeavor. As Kentucky writer Robert Penn Warren noted, the Confederacy became immortal when it died at Appomattox.

*The Library of Virginia*

Confederate Memorial Day in Richmond.

Throughout the decades after the Civil War and into the early 20th century, white Southerners honored the Lost Cause. Confederate veterans became the living embodiments of the cause, telling stories to the young and passing on the meanings of the war effort as they understood them. Politicians interpreted the Lost Cause as a defense of states' rights, and postwar political movements often brought out wartime heroes to give their causes legitimacy. The businesses of the New South era after the war also exploited this sentiment, making Confederate generals honorary, or real, board members to suggest the South's economic interests were in good hands. The most profound and lasting interpretation of the Lost Cause saw its spiritual significance. Defenders of the Lost Cause saw it as a defense of principle itself; a willingness to sacrifice and suffer for one's beliefs. It contrasted Northern materialism and power with Southern honor and principle. Episcopal Bishop Richard Wilmer, of Alabama, wrote, for example, that there were "not only questions of constitutional principle, but deep questions of morals" involved in the war. Presbyterian minister James H. McNeilly argued similarly that the war had been "a war of conscience against conscience — a conflict of moral ideals." He insisted that Northerners had "a perverted conscience" that caused injustice against the South.

The years from 1865 to 1880 were ones of poverty, confusion and disorganization in Southern life. Episcopalian and Confederate veteran Randolph McKim recalled that "When Lee surrendered, the world grew dark to us. We felt as if the sun had set in blood to rise no more." With this initial sense of despondency, about 10,000 Southerners went into exile in 1865, setting up Confederate colonies in Mexico, Brazil and Venezuela. Most white Southerners did not leave, but they became convinced the Confederate defeat jeopardized what they believed to be essentially religious and moral values. The Lost Cause was an assertion that the Confederacy's values would survive the war if Southerners would validate them by affirming the Confederate memory. In the 1880s, the melancholy memorialization of the Confederate dead gave way to a celebration of the war, which lasted through the early decades of the 20th century and saw large crowds at public events honoring the Confederacy.

When a Confederate hero died after the Civil War, the South gave him full honors in ceremonies that mourned the Confederacy's death as well as that of the veteran, reminding true believers of the righteousness of the region's cause and perpetuating the past into the present and future. The "Confederate Veteran's Burial Ritual" emphasized that the soldier was going to "an honorable grave." "He fought a good fight," the ritual said, "and has left a record of which we, his surviving comrades, are proud, and which is a heritage of glory to his family and their descendants, for all time to come." The dedication of monuments to the Confederate heroes also affirmed the cause. In 1914, *Confederate Veteran* magazine revealed that more than a thousand Confederate monuments existed in the South; by that time, many battlefields had been set aside as pilgrimage sites containing essentially holy shrines. Preachers converted the innumerable Confederate statues dotting the Southern landscape into religious objects that quite blatantly taught Christian religious and moral lessons. "Our cause is with God" and "In hopes of a joyful resurrection" were among the most directly religious inscriptions on monuments. The dedication of monuments became more elaborate as time went on. Perhaps the greatest occurred in 1907, when an estimated 200,000 people gathered in Richmond for the dedication of a statue to Jefferson Davis. Virginia Gov. Claude A. Swanson addressed the audience, and 12,000 members of Confederate veterans groups marched in the parade to the site on Monument Avenue, which came to have statues of Stonewall Jackson and Robert E. Lee as well.

Such rituals and places of the Lost Cause celebrated a mythology that focused on the Confederacy as

*The Library of Virginia*

Monument Avenue in Richmond. The statues of Jefferson F. Davis, Robert E. Lee, J.E.B. Stuart, Thomas "Stonewall" Jackson and Matthew F. Maury are erected here. A statue of tennis great Arthur Ashe was placed here in 1996.

The unveiling of J.E.B. Stuart's monument in 1907.

a creation myth. A pantheon of Southern heroes emerged from the farms and plantations of the Old South in the legend, to battle the forces of evil — the Yankees. The Yankee monster symbolized a chaotic, unrestrained Northern society that had threatened the orderly, godly Southern civilization. The myth illustrated the spiritual underpinnings of the Lost Cause, as it replicated the Christian story of Christ's suffering and death, with the Confederacy as the sacred center. The Southern myth of the Lost Cause re-enacted an incomplete Christian drama, though, as there was no redemption for the South; the Confederacy's holy war failed.

Southern ministers portrayed Robert E. Lee, Stonewall Jackson, Jefferson Davis and many other wartime heroes as religious saints and martyrs, epitomizing Christian and Southern values. They identified the Confederate crusade with the virtuous American Revolution, especially by linking George Washington and Lee as the highest

The unveiling of Robert E. Lee's monument in 1890.

products of Southern civilization, said to share religious faith, moral character and superiority to adversity. The images of Confederate heroes pervaded the South and were especially aimed at children. In the early 20th century, United Daughters of the Confederacy (UDC) chapters blanketed Southern schools with portraits of Lee and Davis. Lee's birthday, January 19, became a holiday throughout the South, still celebrated in places as Confederate Heroes Day (and sometimes combined now in Southern states with the celebration of the federal Martin Luther King Jr. holiday). Lee's picture on the wall was the altar for ceremonies. The Protestant South discouraged the display of religious icons as Catholic artifacts, but the likenesses of the Confederate heroes had powerful spiritual overtones. Catholic priest Father Abram Ryan, who wrote melancholy elegies about the Confederacy, was particularly insightful about these images. He told the story of seeing his young niece standing before a painting of Christ on the cross, and he asked her if she knew who had crucified her Lord. "Instantly she replied, 'O yes I know,' she said, 'the Yankees.' "

©*Bradley Schmehl*

Thomas "Stonewall" Jackson

Stained-glass windows in churches commemorated Confederate sacrifices. One of them, in Portsmouth, Virginia, portrayed a biblical Rachel weeping at a tomb, on which appeared the names of congregation members who had died during the Civil War. St. Paul's Episcopal Church in Richmond, which had been the wartime church of many Confederate leaders, put in place a Lee Memorial Window, which used an Egyptian scene to connect the Confederacy with the Old Testament. Wartime artifacts also had a sacred aura about them. The UDC saved the Bible that Jefferson Davis used when sworn in as Confederate president. Museums were sanctuaries containing such sacred relics. The Confederate Museum in Richmond, formerly the White House of the Confederacy, contained a room for each seceding state, each filled with medals, flags, uniforms and weapons from the Confederacy.

The Confederate battle flag became a symbol of the Lost Cause. Gen. P.G.T. Beauregard had reportedly designed the battle flag as a striking symbol that Confederate soldiers could recognize during battle. It was a square red banner, with a blue cross of Saint Andrew, bearing 13 white, five-pointed stars. The Confederate Congress, though, never adopted it as the official flag of the nation, and it never flew over government offices of the Confederate states. Confederate veterans organizations never officially employed the battle flag, either. It nonetheless became a folk symbol associated with the Lost Cause and, more broadly, the South.

*Valentine Museum, Richmond, Virginia*

The unveiling of Stonewall Jackson's monument.

"The Conquered Banner," a postwar poem by Father Abram Ryan, conveyed a reverence for the Confederacy through melancholy lines that saw the flag no longer as a call to arms: "Furl that Banner, softly, slowly. Treat it gently — it is holy — for it droops above the dead."

During Reconstruction after the Civil War, the emblems of the Confederacy took on a charged political meaning, related to the battles for control between the traditional white leadership class of the South and the newly enfranchised African-Americans. The Ku Klux Klan began as a social group among young former Confederate soldiers. Gen. Nathan Bedford Forrest became its first Imperial Wizard, and the link between Lost Cause symbols and white supremacy, thereafter, became stronger than during the war itself. Black Southerners in Reconstruction often used the American flag and the language of democracy and nationalism during ceremonies celebrating their new public life, while white Southerners spoke of their declining fortunes, using a newly refined language of racial control and employing the imagery of the Lost Cause. The wearing of Confederate uniforms or the displaying of the Confederate battle flag was not outlawed by the federal government, but to do either in public activities in the South around 1870 would have marked you as a person of a certain political persuasion — dedicated to restoring white political prerogatives and restricting those of blacks. When Robert E. Lee died in 1870, his family buried him — at his instruction — in a suit, not his wartime uniform, and they displayed neither Confederate nor American flags, all because of his desire not to stir the regional animosities that those symbols provoked.

Certain organizations emerged to promote the perpetuation of the Lost Cause. Confederate veterans groups directed the operations. Local associations of veterans appeared in the 1870s, but the formation of the United Confederate Veterans in 1889 and the United Sons of Confederate Veterans in 1896 injected new energy and organization into what became a social and cultural movement. The highlight of the year for the veterans was the annual region wide reunion, held in a major Southern city. Railroads ran

*©Bradley Schmehl*

Nathan Bedford Forrest

*©Bradley Schmehl*

Robert E. Lee

special trains, and the cities lavishly welcomed the grizzled old men and their entourages of splendidly dressed young women sponsored by local chapters. Tens of thousands of people invaded the chosen city each year. These were social occasions but often also had their religious moments when everyone focused on the reason for the gatherings. The group met in Charleston, South Carolina, in 1899, and a city reporter noted that the veterans were sometimes lighthearted but were also as devout as any pilgrim going "to the tomb of a prophet, or a Christian knight to the walls of Jerusalem."

*Valentine Museum, Richmond, Virginia*

A photograph of the Lee monument during the unveiling of J.E.B. Stuart's monument in 1907.

Women provided even more energy toward ensuring that future generations of Southerners would remember the Lost Cause. Lost Cause spokesmen identified, in the words of Baptist minister and educator J.L.M. Curry, the "purity of our women" with the virtue of Southern civilization itself. The United Daughters of the Confederacy provided an unmatched crusading zeal. The underlying spiritual meaning of the Lost Cause to this group was apparent in the invocation that was a part of the official ritual for their meetings: "Daughters of the Confederacy, this day we are gathered together, in the sight of God, to strengthen the bonds that unite us in a common cause; to renew the vows of loyalty to our sacred principles; to do homage unto the memory of our gallant Confederate soldiers, and to perpetuate the fame of their noble deeds into the third and fourth generations. To this end

*Valentine Museum, Richmond, Virginia*

The Jefferson Davis Monument Association in 1902.

we invoke the aid of our Lord." The group published the "U.D.C. Catechism for Children" in 1912, a title suggesting the sacred qualities they saw in the Lost Cause.

Christian churches also promoted the Lost Cause, believing it taught similar religious moral values as the churches. The God invoked in the Lost Cause was distinctly biblical and transcendent.

*The Library of Virginia*

The Rev. John William Jones

John William Jones, a postwar Baptist minister, often prayed at Confederate veteran gatherings for the blessings of the "God of Israel, God of the centuries, God of our forefathers, God of Jefferson Davis and Sidney Johnston and Robert E. Lee and Stonewall Jackson, God of the Southern Confederacy." Denominational papers approvingly published appeals from Lost Cause organizations for financial support for monument fund raising, recommended Confederate writings and praised the Confederate heroes. The predominant religious tradition of the South has been evangelical Protestantism, reflecting the overwhelming numerical and cultural hegemony of Baptists and Methodists, and Confederate heroes were popular choices to appear at Southern revivals. The most popular post-Civil War evangelist, Georgia Methodist Sam Jones, was a master at having Confederates testify to the power of Christianity in their lives, preferably its inspirational effect on the

battlefield. The invitation to follow Christ was also a summons to once again follow Robert E. Lee, Stonewall Jackson and Jefferson Davis.

The dark side of the Lost Cause, its underlying racial aspect, was seen in the importance of the Ku Klux Klan to it. White Southerners romanticized the Klan as a chivalrous extension of the Confederacy, but it became a terrorist group for white supremacy during Reconstruction. Klansmen used their wartime military connections to spread its influence. The prominence of Confederates in the Klan immediately after the war kept alive the Lost Cause and tied it to the Klan's white supremacy. In 1917, at the unveiling in Pulaski, Tennessee, of a bronze tablet commemorating the birth of the Klan there, a local pastor evoked the religious nature of the organization in his prayer honoring the men "who came from dens and caves in the weird mystery of nightfall to the defense of our rights and homes." The Klan thus entered Southern mythology.

The second Klan emerged in 1915, encouraged by the enormous impact of the film "The Birth of a Nation," which was based on Thomas Dixon Jr.'s racist novel, "The Clansman" (1905). William J. Simmons, an Alabama native and a former Methodist circuit-riding minister, led a contingent of 15 supporters to the top of Stone Mountain, a large granite outcropping east of Atlanta. It became a Confederate monument in the 1920s, with the figures of Lost Cause heroes carved in the granite. Simmons and his disciples gathered stones to make an altar on which they placed an American flag, an unsheathed sword, a canteen of initiation water and a Bible. They also burned a cross of pine boards padded with excelsior and doused with kerosene, a ritual that harked back to ancient practices in the Scottish highlands in Celtic religion. The Klan grew in the 1920s, becoming a political as well as a social and cultural movement, but it was as much associated with promoting "Americanism" as the Lost Cause. The nation

'THE CLANSMAN'
SUPPRESSED

PHILADELPHIA CITIZENS DEMAND RIGHTS IN THE VERY FACE OF TOM DIXON—EX-CONGRESSMAN WHITE PLEADS —DIXON INSULTED MAYOR.

The people throughout the country are particularly interested in the suppression of the Clansman, at Philadelphia, and the Christian Recorder gives a good account of the event.

At last that infamous libel on the Negro race masquerading as a historical drama—"The Clansman," by Thomas Dixon—has been suppressed, at least as far as Philadelphia is concerned. Its suppression is due to the manly courage of a few of the leading colored men of the city who were forced to take what might have appeared as rash methods in their determination to suppress the play. They called upon the people to meet at the theatre Monday night and by their presence to protest against the production of "The Clansman." Fully 3,000 persons responded and so effect’ve was this quiet protest of mere determined presence that the superintendent of public safety asked the leaders to disperse the crowd, assuring them that next morning the mayor would give a full hearing. Promptly at 10 o'clock on Tuesday morning a delegation of our people headed by Dr. N. F. Mossell, presented the matter to the mayor. Our side of it was represented by Revs. Taliferro, of the Baptist church; M. Anderson, of the Presbyterian church; ex-Congressman G. H. White and T. J. Minton, esq. The argument of Congressman White was masterly and evoked an expression of admiration from the mayor. He claimed and sustained the point that

OHS

*Cleveland Journal,*
November 10, 1906.

had embraced the racial and religious outlook of the South by the 1920s, making this convergence possible.

The romantic myth of the Lost Cause told of heroic white Southerners going off to war against Northern aggression, but most black Americans saw Lee and Davis fighting against their freedom. Frederick Douglass, for example, countered the emerging Southern legend of wartime Confederate nobility. "The spirit of secession is stronger today than ever," he wrote in dismay in 1871. "It is now a deeply rooted, devoutly cherished sentiment, inseparably identified with the 'lost cause,' which the half measures of the Government towards the traitors has helped to cultivate and strengthen." Lee's death in 1870 and the eulogies to his character appalled Douglass. "Is it not about time that this bombastic laudation of the rebel chief should cease?" he wrote. Douglass protested the "nauseating flatteries" that newspapers bestowed on Lee. He saw the Lost Cause preventing the South from facing its past of "trading in blood and in the souls of men."

*LIA*

Frederick Douglass

Despite Douglass' words, the Lost Cause took deep root in the post-Civil War South. All of the rituals, institutions and artifacts associated with the Lost Cause helped to nurture and reinforce a social-cultural identity for white Southerners, rooted in their experience of fighting for the Confederacy and remembering it afterward. Historians have pointed out the social divisions within Confederate society, growing out of the different regions and social classes within the South and growing deeper as the war went on and death and sacrifice became common. Those social divisions and resulting conflicts continued after the Civil War, and contention often divided the Lost Cause movement itself as Southerners argued over who was to blame for Confederate battle defeats, criticized Jefferson Davis for his political failures and competed for funds for differing aspects of the Lost Cause. But the Lost Cause became a way for white Southerners to reaffirm a common identity that grew out of the shared bonds of fighting with fellow white Southerners against a common enemy. Defeat in the war had created a spiritual and psychological crisis, raising questions about the continuation of a Southern culture that had grown out of the early settlement of the South. Despite the bafflement and frustration of defeat, white Southerners showed that the time of "creation" still had meaning for them and they invested that identity with spiritual concerns.

Southern celebrants of the Lost Cause came to see the results of the Civil War as a divine rebuke to them. Wartime ministers had claimed that the Confederate cause was a holy war against the infidel North that had embraced licentious liberty. They saw themselves as God's new chosen people. How could the chosen people have lost a holy war? By the 1890s, white Southerners interpreted the results of the war as a rebuke to God's chosen people but not His abandonment of them. Presbyterian cleric James H. McNeilly noted in 1890 that the Bible contained accounts of the Israelites led into captivity by heathen conquerors, "but that fact did not prove the heathen to be right in the cause nor that the Israelites were upholding a bad cause." His conclusion was that "questions of right and wrong before God are not settled by success or defeat of arms." While white Southerners understood Confederate defeat as somehow reflecting their failure to live up to godly ideals, and even admitted they sometimes nurtured slaveowners who might not have been as decent as they should have been, they did not see the Union victory as proof that slavery itself had been inherently wicked. They did accept that the war had destroyed slavery as the South's peculiar institution.

White Southerners looked to the future for vindication of the principles they continued to see as part of their wartime crusade — devotion to duty, standing up for principle, steadfastness of religious belief, the endurance of suffering for a cause. As a poet put it: "From each lost cause of earth, Something precious springs to birth, Tho' lost it be to men, It lives with God again." Presbyterian minister Benjamin Morgan Palmer surmised that "Principles never die, and if they seem to perish it is only to experience a resurrection in the future." Another minister, Moses Drury Hoge, told Southerners in 1889 not to worry about the Confederate cause because future Southern crusaders would "in God's good time vindicate the principles which must ultimately triumph." Confederate defeat came to be seen, then, as a form of discipline from God, preparing the region's people for achievement of ideals in the future.

*The Library of Virginia*

Pastor Robert Lewis Dabney, a Lost Cause minister.

Such an interpretation was part of the early 20th-century Southern belief in a distinctive mission. In a 1909 sermon, Episcopal rector of Saint John's Church in Richmond R.A. Goodwin insisted that "God is in our history as truly as He was in the history of Israel," adding that the defeat of the Confederacy "was a part of the wilderness through which we were led." He saw in 1909 that God had meant for the Southern people's destiny to be a part of the American nation: "Without the welding together of our people by the fiery trials of war, of reconstruction of threatened servile domination we could not have been the conserving power we have been. If this government is still to stand for liberty and freedom it will be the South which will preserve it, and in the good providence of our God, bringing good out of evil, our sufferings will help to bring a blessing to all people." The South's Confederate crusade had not been lost, since a fight for "right and truth and honor" is never lost.

The Lost Cause enabled white Southerners to maintain a culture separate from the rest of the nation's, but reunification with Northerners provided the incentive for Southerners to honor the American nation as well as Southern civilization. The Spanish-American War and World War I provided the perfect context for the South to again embrace the values of the American nation and to show how the Lost Cause was not incompatible with Americanism.

When the Spanish-American War erupted in April 1896, Southern youth enthusiastically joined the war effort. Georgia minister Warren A. Candler insisted that young Southern men would not have marched off to fight for the nation "if Confederate memories had been despised and Confederate history spat upon during all the years since 1865. Visions of heroic sires inflamed the courage of gallant sons." Not all symbols of American nationalism were, to be sure, acceptable. Sumner A. Cunningham, editor of *Confederate Veteran* magazine, led a movement to let Southern soldiers in the United States Army wear brown, rather than blue, uniforms. "Many a noble Confederate who is in blue uniform to-day does not feel as comfortable in it," Cunningham wrote, "as if he did not remember the bitter experiences of 1861-65, and no good can come from continuing to use that color."

Of more substance, white Southerners increasingly at the turn of the 20th century stressed that the Lost Cause had been concerned, in essence, with liberty. Minister H.D.C. Maclachlin insisted in 1909 that secession had been "a sacred duty" because it involved "a question of fundamental human right, or the liberty for which the blood of the Anglo-Saxon had been spilled from the days of the Magna Charta until their own." The association of the Confederacy with the idea of liberty in this period sometimes meant states' rights politics, but sometimes Southerners gave it a broader meaning. Minister P.D. Stephenson claimed that the failed Southern independence movement had ignited "a wave of popular uprisings that for the half-century since intervening has been sweeping over the world." France, the South American nations and the English colonies had all known the birth or extension of liberty; news of impending disturbances in Russia and "the petrified East" also suggested the repercussions of the Confederate embrace of the concept of national independence based in liberty.

The vitality of the Lost Cause, nonetheless, had begun to ebb by World War I. That war represented a landmark in the reincorporation of the South into the Union, and the Lost Cause increasingly came to seem out of date. As time went on in the early 20th century, Lost Cause ceremonies and activities were less likely to evoke spiritual feelings. The pattern of life had changed in the South, and the issues the Lost Cause addressed no longer were of central concern to white Southerners. Lost Cause activities became less and less full community events. The Fourth of July, for example, gradually replaced Confederate Memorial Day as the unifying public holiday of small towns and communities; Lee's birthday was still a holiday, but newspapers only occasionally published editorials about it and attendance at public activities around it declined.

Although the ritualized, institutionalized aspects of the Lost Cause social-cultural movement declined after 1920, the memory of the Confederacy continued to play a role in regional life. Writers continued, for example, to use the Lost Cause in exploring the meaning of the Southern experience. Allen Tate's poem "Ode to the Confederate Dead" in 1926 expressed the frustration of a modern young Southerner standing at the gate of a Confederate cemetery. He thinks of the "inscrutable infantry rising" and of the battles fought. He envies the Confederates, their certainties, their knowledge of why they fought and what they believed. The modern Southerner knows too much, Tate suggests, has too much cultural baggage for simple convictions. He doubts and questions, unable to regain the wholeness of the past. Tate himself tried to regain the certainties of traditional Southern society. He wrote biographies of Stonewall Jackson and Jefferson Davis, read Southern history and toured battle-fields. He sought out an antebellum home with Greek Revival columns, and kept a loaded rifle and a Confederate battle flag over his mantelpiece. He admired the Confederates for battling for a way of life in which they believed, but he was part of what had become a subculture of the South, actively celebrating a tradition that most Southerners had moved beyond in embracing the realities of modern life.

In the 1950s and 1960s, Confederate symbolism re-emerged in the segregationist Lost Cause, a mass movement in response to the Civil Rights movement. Spokesmen for the Lost Cause organizations in the late 19th century had rarely discussed racial issues. Perhaps they simply did not have to do so because the Southern white consensus on racial supremacy was so solid. White Southerners after the Civil War never wanted their memory of the valor of wartime Southerners tainted by associating it with racial issues, even though those had been so central to a war that led to emancipation of African-

Americans from slavery. In any event, the Confederate symbols took on a harsh racial meaning in the 1950s South. Segregationists used the symbols of the Lost Cause, and they became explicitly, almost exclusively, tied in with white supremacy in a new way. Segregationists displayed the Confederate battle flag and sang "Dixie" in protest at Central High School in Little Rock in 1957, at Ole Miss in 1962 and at Selma in 1965. After Central High was successfully integrated, a local official in Forest, Mississippi, ordered the high school band there to play "Dixie" before football games instead of the "Star Spangled Banner." This was powerful symbolism a century after the Civil War. The Ku Klux Klan had made the Confederate battle flag a central symbol, the White Citizens' Councils used it in the 1950s in support of white supremacy, and that remains its prime association in the minds of many Americans. Writer Walker Percy explained the historic shift in meaning in Confederate symbolism and pointed out in 1961 that "racism is no sectional monopoly. Nor was the Confederate flag a racist symbol. But it is apt to be now. The symbol is the same, but the referent has changed. Now when the Stars and Bars flies over a convertible or a speedboat or a citizens' meeting, what it signifies is not a theory of government but a certain attitude toward the Negro."

This phase of the Lost Cause ebbed in the 1970s, with adjustment to the end of legal segregation and less explicit expression of white racism. As a result of the linkage in the 1950s with racial confrontation, the South saw a decline in the display of racial symbolism. Most Southern universities dropped the playing of "Dixie" during sporting events, a practice that was once common throughout the region. After the legal victories against Jim Crow segregation and political disfranchisement in the 1960s, African-Americans began a sharper challenge of the use of Lost Cause symbols as the overall public symbols of the region during the 1970s, beginning a movement that still continues.

The Lost Cause had been a major source of identity for post-Civil War white Southerners, and it was a prominent feature in the public culture of the region. Its symbols became widely associated with the South itself. Playing "Dixie" and showing the Confederate battle flag were recognized ways to evoke "the South" from the end of the Civil War to the 1970s. The ceremonies of Confederate Memorial Day and Robert E. Lee's birthday continued to remind white Southerners of their Confederate heritage, as did the statues honoring the Cause, which still stand on town squares, in cemeteries and on preserved battlefields throughout the South. Black leaders consistently criticized the symbols and rituals of the Lost Cause in the years from 1865 to the 1970s because of their association with the defense of slavery and the Ku Klux Klan's overt use of the Lost Cause to support white supremacy.

The individuals and groups who wanted to honor the bravery and heroism of Confederate soldiers often used the terms "lest we forget" and targeted their efforts of memorialization at the Southern young. They wanted to fix the meaning of the Lost Cause as a spiritual phenomenon above all, one related to regional values. But the race-conscious, socially hierarchal ideologies of the post-Civil War South lay at the base of their memorialization efforts, as well; they never intended that the Lost Cause would speak for active African-American participants in a truly biracial South — which they could not imagine. The eulogists of the Lost Cause from that era might be surprised at the continuing controversies over the display of its symbolism.

The Lost Cause presents, certainly, rousing images of a crusading South, marching off to combat, to the martial strains of "Dixie." It also, though, might have continuing power as a story not for ideologies but of the tragic South, a place of ruins and the very human saga of dashed hopes that resulted from defeat in the Civil War.

# Part III

# Civil War Vapors Remain

by Peter Applebome

ONE AUGUST DAY IN THE SUMMER OF 1999, about 150 Southerners gathered in Flat Rock, North Carolina, at an inn where Confederate soldiers lodged during the Civil War. They sang "Dixie," waved Confederate flags and, declaring the event "the most important day in Southern history since Lee's surrender at Appomatox," hailed the birth of a new political party, the Southern Party. Citing kinship not just with the Confederacy but with independence movements in Quebec, Scotland, Wales and Ireland, they pledged to eventually send enough members to Congress to allow the South to secede again, this time peacefully.

It's entirely possible that one day pigs will fly, cows will learn French and the Confederacy will be born anew, but I don't think I'd bet a lot of money on any of them. In some ways, the gathering, which spawned a grandly rhetorical manifesto dubbed "The Asheville Declaration" ("We the founders of the Southern Party, acting in the spirit of our Southern Colonial and Confederate forefathers ...") was merely a reminder of the triumph of market segmentation. In America, particularly, with the Internet providing ways for left-handed plumbers or South Dakota polka dancers to band together, almost any fringe notion or marginal interest group can coalesce into an organization, if not a movement.

But if the rebirth of the Confederacy is probably not around the corner, that doesn't mean the gathering was without import. Indeed, what's truly striking 135 years after the Grand Review and the end of the Civil War is how much assorted vapors of that period are still with us. The Civil War continues to spawn a never-ending parade of books — more than 60,000 and growing daily — making it by far the most assiduously documented and debated event in American history. In the South, virtually every state in recent years has confronted agonized controversies over imagery of the Civil War. And whether the Confederate flag in South Carolina, the state flag in Mississippi and Georgia, the state song in Virginia or the Confederate statues on Monument Avenue in Richmond, it's astonishing how vital and current the symbols of that era remain. The Confederate flag even became a major issue in the 2000 Republican presidential race.

It's easy to dismiss this as a peculiarly Southern fixation, a reminder of the way that it's the losers of wars who cling to history with the greatest ferocity. And there is something stereotypically Southern about it, like a parody of the old saw about saving your Dixie cups because the South will rise again. But it would be a huge mistake to think there's just a Southern eccentricity at work. And like Mississippi writer William Faulkner's famous remark that "the past is never dead. It isn't even past," what's most telling about the Civil War is how much it reflects unresolved issues in American life. As James M. McPherson pointed out in his "Battle Cry of Freedom," the Civil War made us what we are. Before 1861, we said the United States "are" — it was the individual states that dominated, not their union. Afterward, we said the United States "is." Similarly, before the war, even in Abraham Lincoln's speeches, there were constant references to the Union, as if the agreement of the states to unite was still a salient issue. After the war, we talked of the nation, as if the union of states was simply of historical interest.

But if the Civil War made us the nation we are, that nation is hardly a unified one that speaks in a single voice. In many ways, the prosperity at the turn of the century has smoothed over the differences in American life. These days, it seems, the only party that really matters is the one thrown by the Dow and NASDAQ. But beneath the pacific hum of prosperity at the century's end is a nation where many of the issues that divided North and South 135 years ago still divide us, and where many of the cultural divides that made North and South, for a time, function as two separate nations still exist. So looking back toward the euphoria of the Grand Review and the historic reunification it celebrated, it's worth asking two questions. The first is, what issues still linger from those days and how do we address them? The second is, how much of a unification do we really want?

The answer to the first question is that 135 years after the Civil War, it's striking how much remains unresolved — in terms of race, in terms of our view of the federal government, in terms of the role of religion in American life. If the Civil War reflected, in many ways, not just two armies but two world views, many of the wounds have yet to heal. And if some of those scars reflect divisions of geography — North and

> It's easy to dismiss this as a peculiarly Southern fixation, a reminder of the way that it's the losers of wars who cling to history with the greatest ferocity.

South still are different places — a lot of them are not so simple. Against all evidence to the contrary, for example, we still cling to the notion of racial ills as essentially the province of the South. So healing the wounds of the past has to begin with two potentially contradictory thoughts — that many regional differences still linger, and that when it comes to race, our sins are national, not regional.

The answer to the second dilemma is more elusive and it's inextricably linked to the first. If one challenge to the nation is to heal the wounds from a divided America, another, paradoxically, is to find a way to nurture and maintain the regional distinctiveness and cultural differences that in some ways gave rise to the war. We don't want to be a divided nation. But we don't want to be a totally homogeneous one, either. And healing the wounds may come more naturally than respecting the differences that gave rise to them.

The schisms in American life are no longer as geographically neat as they were 135 years ago (although, of course, there were plenty of Unionists in the South and plenty of Northerners either perfectly content to see the South go its own way or perfectly comfortable with the institution of slavery). And in a nation that now stretches to the Pacific, not just the Mississippi, North versus South seems an inherently limited window for viewing the nation.

But if it's true that North and South no longer defines all the pressure points in American life, the cultural and political fault lines in American life still have a distinctly regional tinge, with Southern conservatives dominating the Republican Party and the religious right, and with moderates and liberals, most of them outside the South, dominating the Democrats. If there's still a North-South divide in American life, it should be no surprise. The country was founded amid an uneasy peace between North and South, so profound that many of the founding fathers wondered whether two regions so different could form a genuine union. It was Northern states that first seriously pondered secession, beginning with a threat to secede in 1803 if Louisiana were purchased, and flickering on and off for years afterward. From the 1820s until the Civil War, the regional split, particularly over whether to extend slavery to the Western territories, defined the nation's politics. As late as the 1930s, the Northern writer Carl Carmer could venture to Alabama and come away thinking he had gone to a foreign land. "The Congo," he wrote, "is not more different from Massachusetts or Kansas or California" than those states are different from Alabama. And as recently as the 1960s, the civil rights revolution and the efforts of the federal courts to end segregation in the South produced perhaps the most bitter domestic battle of the 20th century.

Carmer's observation may have been an overstatement then, and it's certainly one now. But it's not entirely divorced from reality, either. North and South are still different. It's worth remembering that from the nation's founding to the Civil War, two-thirds of the Presidents were slaveholding Southerners, and by pretty much the same margin, the South dominated the Supreme Court and the top positions in the Congress. Then came the war and a Union victory that produced politics even more dominated by the North than they had been by the South. It took another full century for a politician (Lyndon Johnson) representing a state that had been a member of the Confederacy to be elected President, and it took half a century to have a House Speaker or President Pro Tem of the Senate from a Southern state. But over the last third of the 20th century, the South came again to dominate American politics. Republicans, without question, have their base in the South, and their political successes, from the days of Nixon to the presidency of George Bush, reflected a Southern strategy of, above all else, catering to white Southerners, who were in the process of converting from loyal Democrats to solid Republicans. Democrats have not elected a President without a Southerner on the ticket since the days of FDR. And when they finally re-elected one, it was with two Southerners on the ticket. For much of Bill Clinton's administration, the President, Vice President, House Speaker, House Majority Leader, House Majority Whip and Senate Majority Leader were all Southerners. Indeed, when the Senate Majority Leader post came open when Bob Dole decided to run for President in 1996, the two contenders were Trent Lott and Thad Cochran from Mississippi, the most Southern state of them all.

And, if no regions speak in a single voice, Southerners (or at least white ones) in positions of political power tend to espouse remarkably consistent positions. They tend to favor, at least in theory, the power of the states over the power of the federal government (except when it comes to getting their share of the federal pie), prayer in schools and a general tolerance for a greater public role for religion than now exists. They tend to favor stricter controls on immigration, they side with gun owners over gun-control forces, pro-life forces over pro-choice ones, and favor fiscal curbs such as the balanced-budget amendment and whatever the issue is of the moment that defines social conservatism and the right-hand side of the values divide.

Most of the precise issues salient now were unknown 135 years ago, but on issues such as the role of religion in political life and the balance of power between the states and the federal government, their views are remarkably consistent with their Confederate forebearers. Indeed, if there were fundamental philosophical differences between the Confederacy and the Union, aside from slavery, they had to do with issues of religion in public life and the balance of power between the states and the federal government. This is not to say today's Southern politicians are closet Confederates. (Although Trent Lott himself once declared that the fundamental principles that Jefferson Davis believed in, such as smaller government and conservative values, are the fundamental principles of the Republican Party). It is to say that an understanding of American life and politics has to take into account the degree to which the divisions between North and South are still very real and are likely to remain that way. It seems like a long time since the angry-white-male moment of 1994, when Southern conservatives managed to galvanize the nation and engineered the Republican takeover of Congress based on an agenda that came down to states' rights and conservative values. The political moment faded quickly. But there's still a deep divide on issues of values, on the balance of power between the states and the federal government, over abortion, prayer in schools and big government whose nexus has a distinctly regional bent. And if it's a split that was distinctly muted at the fat-and-happy turn of the century, it's likely to resurface when the economy eventually turns down. Issues of race, of immigration, of values, over who gets what share of the pie inevitably turn harsher when the pie seems smaller, as it inevitably will sooner or later.

Conversely, to return to the paradoxical thought, if it's essential to recognize lingering regional differences, it's equally essential to be able to see through them, particularly on race. Southern historians have long debated the theme of Southern distinctiveness. What is it that makes the South different and what role does the South's oppositional quality play for the nation as

> The gravest wound of America's past and of the Civil War remains that of race. But it's a collective sin, a national failure.

a whole? C. Vann Woodward, the great Southern historian who did his most famous work at Yale in the 1950s and 1960s, has famously laid out the case for the South as a place with an experience alien to most Americans — the experience of defeat in a land that knew only victory; the experience of guilt over slavery in a nation defined by a sense of innocence and a democratic, egalitarian ethos; the experience of poverty in a land of plenty — a place consumed with the past in a nation always rushing pell-mell into the future.

The differences are real to a degree, but, as Woodward himself pointed out, deceptive as well. To take race alone, the North had slavery until it died out for economic reasons. Northern businessmen, not Southerners, ran and profited from the slave trade. Throughout the 19th century, a sense of white supremacy was as endemic in the North as the South. When he made his famous voyage across America in 1831 and '32, the French historian and political philosopher Alexis de Tocqueville observed: "The prejudice of race appears to be stronger in the states that have abolished slavery than in those where it still exists." Lincoln himself repeatedly affirmed his aversion to any notion of racial equality and in his famous letter to the abolitionist Horace Greeley wrote, "If I could save the Union without freeing any slave, I would do it, and if I could save it by freeing all the slaves I would do it." After the war, North and South turned their backs on the freed slaves and joined in a consensus that, as the historian Kenneth M. Stampp put it: "The Civil War was America's glory and reconstruction her disgrace." More recently, it was Northern cities that burned in the racial riots of the 1960s. The most segregated school systems remain in places such as Chicago and Boston. The racial atrocities of the moment are at least as likely to happen in New York City or Los Angeles as Jasper, Texas.

The point is not to let the South off the hook for its failings on race or for the indelible stain of slavery. No sins of race weigh heavier on the nation's soul than slavery or Jim Crow or the bombs and attack dogs of Birmingham. Instead, it's to remember that the idea of a fallen, racist, benighted South served to deflect the rest of the nation from an honest scrutiny of itself. As long as the South was the repository of evil on race, the rest of the nation could be seen as the repository of virtue — just as history has often cast the Civil War in a virtuous, wildly oversimplified glow as a war to free the slaves. Or as Woodward put it in 1962: "The South has long served the nation in ways still in great demand. It has been a moral lightning rod, a deflector of national guilt, a scapegoat for stricken conscience. It has served the country as much as the Negro has served the white supremacist — as a floor under self-esteem."

The notion still lives, for instance, in the way that Hollywood turns time and again to the images out of the old South, of pot-bellied sheriffs, of gap-toothed Klansmen, of murderous, leering rednecks as our convenient symbols of American racism, leaving the subtler, more pervasive forms to fester in peace. And if there's any notion that deserves a final burial on the anniversary of the Grand Review, it's that when it comes to race, we have met the enemy — and it is they, namely, the fallen South. To whatever degree the Civil War was a war to free the slaves — and you can

> Indeed, what's truly striking 135 years after the Grand Review and the end of the Civil War is how much assorted vapors of that period are still with us.

argue that one forever — it was not a war to guarantee equality in any form for African-Americans. We came closest to waging that war for a few fitful years in the 1960s, but that era was short-lived as well. The gravest wound of America's past and of the Civil War remains that of race. But it's a collective sin, a national failure. And a true reconciliation has to begin with a recognition that the sins of race play out on both sides of the Mason-Dixon Line and on both sides of the Mississippi. Malcolm X once observed that, "As far as I am concerned, Mississippi is anywhere south of the Canadian border." And a fair reading of the legacy of the war has to take into account the shameful treatment of the freedmen after the war as much as the end of slavery.

On the other hand, maybe the real hurdle now isn't regional rapprochement. It's maintaining a sense of regionalism at all. We seem to be galloping into the new millennium — or, depending on your accounting, the year leading up to it — by embracing the future so ardently that it's almost impossible to keep in mind the past. The reigning national stereotype of the moment is that we are more than ever before a mass culture, not a regional one. And, it's often argued, that if you go to the suburbs of Boston or the suburbs of Atlanta, or Des Moines or Sacramento, you're in pretty much the same place, an interchangeable empire of Bennigan's and Old Navy and Starbucks and Home Depot. Maybe we don't need to worry about healing old wounds because commerce has made them mere curiosities of the past. Maybe looking back to the Grand Review, in the end, is all about the past and nothing about the present.

In a time of peace and prosperity, when technology promises to make more of us rich than ever seemed possible, it's a seductive vision. It's also an utterly wrongheaded one. Just as the north of France and the south of France or Northern Italy and Southern Italy are fundamentally different places, America remains a country with many different hearts beating just beneath the surface. It's no accident that regionalism is suddenly a hot topic in universities, regional encyclopedias are being cranked out for the South, New England, the Great Plains, the American West and cities such as New York and Chicago. The National Endowment for the Humanities, under William Ferris of Mississippi, is moving to create centers around the nation to nurture and support local literature, music, arts, crafts, folkways, food and approaches to politics, urbanism and planning.

We look back to the Civil War, the greatest tragedy in American history, to see where we went wrong and to ponder how much of it we've made right since. But we also look back to remember what a vast, multi-hued quilt we evolved from and what deep and rich furrows there are in the national terrain. And one way to pay our respect to the men who fought and died and to the magnitude of the suffering is to respect the differences that still shimmer beneath the surface of our national life. The worst way to mark the Grand Review would be to hail some bland sort of national unanimity devoid of messy bits of unfinished business such as Confederate heritage groups, Northern ghettos, segregated schools and continuing racial disparities North and South, even the Southern Party. We need to heal the wounds. But we need just as much to take note of the differences that long ago made us what we are and still keep us that way. In the fractures that tore our nation apart 140 years ago, we can still see ourselves reflected in ways that matter very much today.

# Part IV

# United We Stand

by L. Douglas Wilder

THE THEME OF THE 135TH ANNIVERSARY OF THE GRAND REVIEW, "Healing Our Nation," suggests that there is an illness afflicting America that requires our focused attention. We assume that most Americans recognize that there was or is a divide that causes the nation's health to be brought into question. If America is ill, we must submit these United States to a diagnosis, to identify the disease and its symptoms; a prognosis, the forecast of the course of the disease; and a cure. If a sickness is determined, then every American must be responsible for finding the cure, including a remedy for the long-term effects and sometimes fatal consequences of racism on our nation.

Facing problems is America's strength. The nation's history is steeped in its people rallying around a problem until it is resolved. And when America does that, the world takes notice.

Prior to the new millennium, the country stood with great apprehension and grave concern about one certain aspect of our nation's well-being. The diagnosis was of a high-tech malady. The prognosis was that our beloved computers might trigger dire consequences and threaten our quality of life by failing to accurately distinguish the year 2000 from the year 1900. The cure: Retrograde and retool the giant computer complexes. This preventive medicine made for an easy transition into the new century and assured our continued well-being as world leader.

America showed that it could overcome that problem and not allow our nation to fall victim to the demons of Y2K. We accepted the challenge, rallied our forces and dealt with the problem. Did we overreact by spending too much money, or were we just lucky? What about nations that did virtually nothing in the face of the expected problem, yet came through it unscathed as well? Who really had the answer? I know one thing: The American people were united in believing that we should err on the side of caution and be prepared. That type of commitment is what makes this country of ours so special. But do we burn with the same intensity on the issue of the "perennial divide," which is not just one of race but of all the issues that divide us, such as age, gender, religion and ethnicity? Have we accepted the responsibility for finding a cure?

Each year, beginning in January with the celebration of the Dr. Martin Luther King Jr. holiday and continuing into February's African-American History Month observances, many people cock an ear and listen to the problems along the racial divide. With solemnity and purpose, they summon the will to focus on the dream and the dreamer, and they cite the unfinished agenda. Death and the passage of time do wonders for great reflection.

We are still a young nation, and our accomplishments and leadership among nations belie our relatively short existence. We are not yet 225 years old, and the fact that we have come this distance after almost being torn asunder during the Civil War, prior to our real maturity, is truly amazing. But there is still the unfinished business of removing the vestiges of division and acknowledging the need for healing. The leadership of "good doctors" is crucial, and if we are to find a cure, the healers' qualifications must include courage, wisdom and the willingness to engage in understanding dialogue.

Our nation has many pent-up energies and emotions that we must deal with as we pursue democratic principles and ideals. At the start of the 20th century, the educator, historian and civil rights leader W.E.B. DuBois stated that America's problem is "the problem of the color line." Historian Arthur M. Schlessinger Jr. predicts that DuBois' prophecy will come into its own in this century. Many Americans still seek full participation in all that this country has to offer. They have experienced years of denial and of doors being slammed in their faces, years of cross burnings and violence. And the result has been protest and even more violence.

The movement against white racism took a long time to gather steam. There have been sincere efforts to address the wrongs, but the wheels of change turn slowly, and patience has become a necessary part of the cure. Alexis de Tocqueville, the French statesman and student of the American political system, explained the problem: "Patiently endured so long as it seemed beyond redress, a grievance comes to appear intolerable once the possibility of removing it crosses men's minds. For the mere fact that certain abuses have been remedied draws attention to others, and they now appear more galling; people may suffer less, but their sensibility is exacerbated."

Schlessinger notes that though the problem of DuBois' color line remains, the

> We are not yet 225 years old, and the fact that we have come this distance after almost being torn asunder during the Civil War, prior to our real maturity, is truly amazing.

affliction is not the rejection of the white majority by minorities but rather the rejection of minorities by the white majority.

The pain and anguish resulting from the diametric positions of the defenders of flying the Confederate flag and those who know what it has come to symbolize are difficult to explain to those who have not been involved in the efforts of the two camps. Tensions simmer as that battle flag flies over the state capitol of South Carolina and enjoys a place on the state flag of Georgia. Yet I take comfort in knowing, particularly in the Commonwealth of Virginia, that those taut feelings of angst dissipate more and more with each passing day, month and year. And it is not simply because the planet is getting older. The change has resulted from the efforts of the too often relative few who are struck by what is and what ought to be.

We have been fortunate in our experiment with democracy, but we need an assessment of our progress and our pace. We will not have the same luxury of time that we had in the last century. We have to learn to deal with a highly technological world and its brand-new problems.

Many compare this time of change with the Industrial Revolution, which eliminated archaic jobs as it fostered new types of work. The computer revolution eliminates the need for many old and inefficient forms of labor. But it also strengthens class barriers and creates rigid new ones, particularly between the well-educated and the poorly educated. The gap between the haves and the have-nots grows wider. This change brings tension, which gives rise to unrest in homes and neighborhoods and even our schools.

We should not allow the 135th anniversary of the Grand Review to pass without sending the message that though we are a nation of laws and not of men, our situation might be considered a logical fallacy. Men have made the laws, implemented them and interpreted them. And laws do not exist separate from social agenda or historical context. We have dismantled the laws that denied the right to vote. We have changed the interpretation of the law that required "separate but equal." In the Fourteenth Amendment, we defined citizenship for the first time, and we chose due process as the guideline for our rights.

Is the nation sick? What, exactly, is the malady? What are the symptoms? Is it infectious or communicable? What therapeutics have been tried? And what has been the impact of our various interventions?

In war, we treat the illness with a scalpel. In peace, we can use negotiation and public policy to bring about healing.

During the celebration of the 135th anniversary of the Grand Review, this message seems truly fitting: Men fought a war and caused a nation of laws to be built. That war is over, and it need never be fought again. We are at that point in our history when we can look to the past and learn from our mistakes. We must lay claim to our nation's greatness and do all that is possible to ensure against harm and protect for future generations even greater opportunities.

We are a nation of many races, religions, cultures and heritages. It is the unity of our variety that makes us great. We are not perfect, and we continually err. But I am optimistic that our nation's ideals can be achieved. I am convinced that Americans of good will can and will prevail against the bigots of all races, the zealots who selfishly promote themselves, the naysayers who can't see progress and the hate mongers who try to slow that progress.

Let us all lay claim to America. We have seen her sons and daughters of all races, creeds, religions and colors join in defending and fighting for what Lincoln described as the "last best hope on Earth." We have witnessed the tearing down of walls that separate and divide Americans. Though there is much to be done, we have seen persons of various colors and ethnicities, as well as women, come to occupy some of the most important and powerful positions in the land. The noted historian Theodore H. White wrote: "Had a satellite from space been circling the Earth every 10 years since the coming of the colonists to North America, it would have beamed back a startling panorama of change. But no more significant change would have shown than in the belt of land between the 49th parallel and the Southern gulfs, which came to be known as the United States.

"The satellite would have shown first the impelling of the forest, the murmuring of the pines and the hemlocks along the Atlantic Shore, then clearing of the hardwoods that have forested both slopes of the Appalachians. Then would have followed the squaring of the green prairies and plains into sections and quarter sections, then the speckling of the valleys and villages that grew into cities. Then the tracery of iron rails linking east and west coasts, until finally, in 1890, the satellite would have shown that the entire country below was so traced by the marks of men that there was no longer any frontier of settlement."

What I find interesting about this observation is the recognition of change. The only thing that is constant is change. And despite the cries from those who pine for the "good old days," there never have been good days for all of America's people because of the barriers of race, class, age and gender.

America has the great minds to tackle this problem, but on many occasions we find the very taproots of our society to be malignant with greed, corruption, selfishness and exploitation. I am not delivering a jeremiad, but I am saying we must recognize the causes of our problems. That task becomes more difficult when there is increasing loss of respect for the things that we hold to be venerable.

Our commitment in some arenas has been absolute. During the Cold War, we spent billions to keep the "Evil Empire" from encroaching on the institutions and

> We have been fortunate in our experiment with democracy, but we need an assessment of our progress and our pace. We will not have the same luxury of time that we had in the last century.

nations that had started experiments with democracy. And though some questioned the burgeoning defense budgets, the anticipated crumbling of the Soviet Union united the American people in the belief that the threat had to be dealt with.

I find that same sense of purpose and urgency to be absent as we seek to live out our creed and hold high the beacon to other nations. I humbly submit that we will not find our commitment by continuing to joust over who is good and who is bad in our society, and I say that particularly in relation to religion and political party affiliation.

Nor will we reach that point with the broad strokes of some executive's pen, some court's decision or some legislative act. While those actions have helped to bring us to where we are in our deliverance, much more is required for us to truly address the problems of the last century and the present. We must reach further, because only by respecting and protecting the rights of every American can any American, with providential blessings, be able to guarantee to his or her posterity the beauty and bounty of this land. I am certain that there are far more things that unite us than divide us, and our dialogue must be never-ending.

It would indeed be tragic if we allowed the fratricide to continue. It has gone on far too long. Even without the arms of war and the declaration thereof, the casualty toll mounts. Whether at Columbine or Los Angeles, Charleston or New York, the divide is there.

The glow we see on America's horizon is the glimmer of either twilight or dawn. The responsibility and the challenge are great, but the resilience and resourcefulness of the American people are greater. And this time around, we cannot blame it on our stars, for as Marc Antony said to Brutus, the fault is in ourselves.

# Part V

# The National Civil War Museum

THE NATIONAL CIVIL WAR MUSEUM in Harrisburg, Pennsylvania, is more than the study and presentation of history. It is dedicated to the preservation of our great American democracy and the ideals on which the nation was founded. The museum is intended to teach young and old about who we are as a people and a country, tracking modern society to the cataclysm of the Civil War. One will find that, in most ways, the Americans today are not much different than those who lived 140 years ago. In fact, the resemblance can be uncanny.

Unlike many Civil War museums, The National Civil War Museum is national in scope, including both the Confederacy and the Union in its exhibits. The National Civil War Museum also has exhibits on slavery. It is impossible to tell the whole story of the Civil War without including the issue of slavery.

The museum inventory is as varied as it is extensive. The results of nearly six years of acquisitions, the collection has a significant number of one-of-a-kind historical items, many never before seen by the public or scholars.

Acquiring the collection proved to be an arduous and tedious task. Many of the items came from direct descendants of ordinary as well as major Civil War figures, usually through a dealer.

The museum has Gen. Robert E. Lee's gloves, some of his maps and the Bible he carried from the Mexican-American War through the fall of Petersburg, Virginia, in 1865.

The only major collection of Gen. George Pickett's memorabilia is also owned by the museum and is a key part of its Gettysburg exhibit.

Union Brig. Gen. Joshua Lawrence Chamberlain was a prolific letter writer, and many of his notes — including ones from just after his July 2, 1863, defense of Little Round Top at Gettysburg as the colonel of the 10th Maine Regiment — are held by the museum.

There are items used and owned by Gen. Ulysses S. Grant and President Abraham Lincoln as well as an unidentified Confederate general's

The National Civil War Museum

uniform. Also on display will be the uniform worn by a Union soldier on the night he allowed John Wilkes Booth to leave Washington after Lincoln's assassination.

The National Civil War Museum is situated in Reservoir Park, the highest point in Harrisburg City. The site was selected because of its grassy and rolling terrain. The structure, at more than 60,000 square feet and two stories high, is crowned by a cupola and has an interior rotunda. The museum gift shop may be the most extensive in the country.

The National Civil War museum provides a thoughtful and comprehensive format to tell the America of today how it came to be. It is a study of our society, our diversity and our democracy, reflected from the epoch of our Civil War. It is a gift to the nation that we may know and understand our past — and ourselves — and so that we may therefore forge a better future for ourselves as one people and one country.

— Stephen R. Reed,
Mayor of Harrisburg

Museum artifacts photographed by
Dane Hildebrand.

# Ulysses S. Grant's Sword Belt

*LIA*

# John White Geary, Presentation Sword

LC

Geary was born in Mount Pleasant, Pennsylvania, on December 30, 1819. He was commander of the 115th Field Artillery. He saw action at Chancellorsville, Gettysburg, Lookout Mountain and was with Gen. William T. Sherman during the Atlanta Campaign. He was promoted to major general while military governor of Savannah, Georgia. In 1866, he was elected to the first of two consecutive terms as Republican governor of Pennsylvania. He was buried with state honors in Harrisburg Cemetery in Harrisburg, Pa.

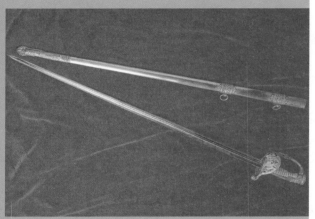

# Alexander S. Webb, Presentation Sword

Webb was born into a prominent New York family in 1835. His grandfather had been on George Washington's staff during the Revolutionary War. Webb graduated from West Point in 1855. In the first two years of the Civil War, he worked with various generals. At the battle of Spotsylvania in May 1864, he was struck by a bullet that passed through the corner of his right eye and came out his ear. He survived the wound and returned in the last months of the war as the Army of the Potomac's chief of staff.

*LC*

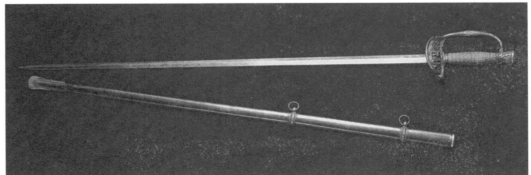

# Robert E. Lee's Gauntlets

©Bradley Schmehl

# James Ewell Brown (J.E.B.) Stuart's Presentation Sword

Born in 1833 in Patrick City, Virginia, Stuart attended West Point. He spent years in Kansas on frontier duty. In 1859, he traveled east to sell the War Department the rights to an invention of his — a device to hold a cavalry saber to the belt. In May 1861, Stuart resigned his Army commission and accepted a commission as lieutenant colonel in the Virginia infantry.

Stuart became known as the "Cavalier of Dixie" during the Civil War. He was Robert E. Lee's "eyes of the army." Stuart was mortally wounded on May 11, 1864, at Yellow Tavern. He died the next day. (The sword Stuart is holding in this picture is the one on display at the museum.)

*LIA*

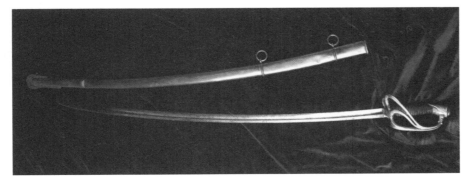

# Zouave Jacket

In the Crimean and the 1859 Franco-Austrian wars, the French Army Zouaves became famous for their bravery and for their strange, colorful uniforms. Officially organized in 1831 in Algeria and composed of tribesmen from Zouaoua, the Zouaves eventually admitted Europeans into their ranks. The original Zouave uniform had white leggings, baggy red pants, a blue sash, a dark blue vest, a red cap trimmed short, a dark blue jacket and a blue-tasseled red fez that for dress was wrapped with a green turban.

The Zouaves influenced the formation of similar units in the United States. Probably the first U.S. unit, the U.S. Zouave Cadets, was organized in Chicago. Later, in New York, another Zouave unit was formed, composed of firemen. When the Civil War began, many of these American Zouave units, which had originally been organized for drill competition, volunteered to fight. Because of the colorful uniforms, the Zouaves made good targets on the battlefield, but the units did not discard their distinctive outfits.

The name Samuel Postern of an unknown regiment was found stitched inside the jacket.

# The Bugle

Every Union regiment was assigned "field musicians." As a rule, fifers or drummers went to infantry units and buglers to cavalry units. The sounds produced by the instruments orchestrated tactical movements on the battlefield.

When assembled into a drum corps, the field musicians became the clocks to which soldiers reacted. An historian of the 17th Maine wrote: "As the first beam of the rising sun begins to tinge the eastern skies, the clear notes of the bugle sounding reveille from headquarters are heard — repeated in turn by the regimental buglers. The drums of one regiment commence their noisy rataplan, which is taken up by another, till

every drum corps of the brigade, which accompanying bugles and fifes, joins in the din, and the morning air is resonant with the rattle of the drum, the shrill notes of the fife, or the clarion tones of the bugle."

# The Slouch Hat

The practical soldier preferred a wide-brimmed slouch hat. This style of hat was popularized by Louis Kossuth, a renowned Hungarian patriot who visited the United States in 1851. The hat shown here was worn by a member of the 3rd Cavalry. The unit is unknown.

# Military Uniforms

Note the stitching detail on the collar.

Sergeant's short jacket, possibly from a Northern state militia.

Staff Eagle Button

Frock coat, pants and kepi of Lt. James McGinley of the 69th Pennsylvania.

Frock coat belonging to Confederate Gen. George Maney.

# The Colt Handgun

Shortly after the start of the Civil War, the citizens of Ashby, Massachusetts, agreed to provide each volunteer with a Bowie knife, a Bible, $10 and a revolver.

The federal government, however, was not convinced that Samuel L. Colt's handguns would be effective in war. So it issued handguns only to cavalry men and mounted light artillerymen. Infantry volunteers who wanted a sidearm had to provide their own.

Many soldiers also lacked confidence in the sidearm. "Pistols are useless," wrote a major of the 2nd Michigan Cavalry. "I have known regiments that have been in the field over two years that never used their pistols in action. At a charge, the saber is the weapon."

The U.S. government purchased 373,077 handguns during the Civil War. The revolvers of choice were the Colt and Remington models known as Army .44 caliber.

To load the percussion six-shooter, the hammer was half-cocked, freeing the cylinder. Ammunition was dropped into each chamber and tamped with the rammer stored under the barrel.

# Selected Bibliography

(For the Grand Review story)

Alfriend, Frank H. *Life of Jefferson Davis.* 1867.

Angle, Paul M., ed. *Three Years in the Army of the Cumberland: The Letters and Diary of Major James A. Connolly.* New York: Indiana University Press, 1969.

Baker, Jean H. *Mary Todd Lincoln, A Biography. New York*: W. W. Norton & Co., 1987.

Bates, David Homer. *Lincoln in the Telegraph Office.* New York: The Century Co., 1907.

Brooks, Noah. *Washington, D.C. In Lincoln's Time.* Chicago: Quadrangle Books, Inc., 1971.

Carpenter, Francis Bicknell. *The Inner Life of Abraham Lincoln, Six Months at the White House.* Boston: The Riverside Press, Cambridge, 1883.

Catton, Bruce. *Grant Takes Command.* Boston: Little, Brown and Co., 1969.

Chamberlain, Joshua L. *The Passing of the Armies ... .*Ohio: Morningside Bookshop, 1982.

Cleaves, Freeman. *Meade of Gettysburg.* Oklahoma: University of Oklahoma Press, 1960.

Crozier, Emmet. *Yankee Reporters.* Oxford University Press, 1956.

Dana, Charles A. *Recollections of the Civil War.* New York: D. Appleton and Co., 1898.

Davis, Burke. *Sherman's March.* Random House, 1980.

Davis, Kenneth C. *Don't Know Much About the Civil War.* New York: William Morrow and Co., Inc., 1996.

DeGregorio, William A. *The Complete Book of U.S. Presidents.* New York: Wings Books, 1993.

Donald, David H. *Lincoln.* New York: Simon & Schuster, 1995.

Downey, Fairfax. *Famous Horses of the Civil War.* New York: Thomas Nelson & Sons, 1959.

Ezell, John S. *The South Since 1865.* New York: The Macmillian Co., 1963.

Fellman, Michael. *Citizen Sherman, A life of William T. Sherman.* New York: Random House, 1995.

Fitch, Michael Hendrick. *Echoes of the Civil War as I Hear Them.* R. F. Fenno & Co., 1905.

Flower, Frank Abial. *Edwin McMasters Stanton, The Autocrat of Rebellion, Emancipation and Reconstruction.* Ohio: The Saalfield Publishing Co., 1905.

Glatthaar, Joseph T. *The March to the Sea and Beyond: Sherman's Troops in the Savannah and Carolinas Campaigns.* New York: New York University Press, 1985.

Gorham, George C. *Life and Public Service of Edwin M. Stanton.* 2 vols. 1899.

Grant, Ulysses S., *Personal Memoirs of U. S. Grant ... .* E. B. Long, ed., New York: paperback ed., Da Capo Press, 1982. Originally published New York: C.L. Webster & Co., 2 vols., 1885-1886.

Halsey, Ashley, ed. *A Yankee Private's Civil War by Robert Hale Strong.* Chicago: Henry Regnery Co., 1961.

Hatcher, Edmund N. *The Last Four Weeks of War.* Ohio: Co-operative Publication Co., 1891.

Hedley, Fenwick Y. *Marching Through Georgia ... .* 1890.

Hendrick, Burton J. *Lincoln's War Cabinet.* Boston: Little, Brown and Co., 1946.

Patricia L. Faust, ed. *Historical Times Illustrated Encyclopedia of the Civil War.* New York: Harper Perennial, 1986.

Holloway, Laura C. *Howard The Christian Soldier.* New York: Funk & Wagnalls , 1885.

Horan, James, D. *Mathew Brady, Historian with a Camera.* New York: Bonanza Books, 1955.

Howe, M.A. DeWolfe, ed. *Home Letters of General Sherman.* New York: Charles Scribner's Sons, 1909.

Hyman, Harold M. and Thomas, Benjamin P. *Stanton, The Life and Times of Lincoln's Secretary of War.* New York: Alfred A. Knopf, 1962.

Johnston, Joseph E. *Narrative of Military Operations.* 1874.

Jones, Katharine M. *When Sherman Came: Southern Women and the "Great March."* New York: The Bobbs-Merrill Co. Inc., 1964.

Keckley, Elizabeth. *Behind the Scenes. Or, Thirty Years a Slave, and Four Years in the White House.* New York: Oxford University Press, 1988. Originally published New York: G.W. Carlton, 1868.

Lewis, Lloyd. *Myths of Lincoln.* New York: The Readers Club, 1941.

Lewis, Lloyd. *Sherman: Fighting Prophet.* New York: Harcourt, Brace and Co., Inc., 1932.

Marszalek, John F. *Sherman's Other War. The General and the Civil War Press.* Memphis State University Press, 1981.

Marszalek, John F. *Sherman: A Soldier's Passion for Order.* New York: Free Press, 1993.

McAllister, Anna. *Ellen Ewing, Wife of General Sherman.* New York: Benziger Brothers, 1936.

McPherson, James M. *Ordeal By Fire: The Civil War and Reconstruction.* New York: Knopf, 1982.

McPherson, James M. *The Negro's Civil War*. New York: Ballantine Books, 1991.

McClellan, George B. *McClellan's Own Story ... .* New York: Charles L. Webster & Co., 1887.

Merrill, James M. *William Tecumseh Sherman*. Chicago: Rand McNally, 1971.

Panzer, Mary. *Mathew Brady and the Image of History*. Smithsonian Institution Press, 1997.

Porter, Horace. *Campaigning with Grant*. New York: Century, 1897.

Randall, James G. and Donald, David H. *The Civil War and Reconstruction*. 2nd, Boston: D. C. Heath and Co., 1961.

Randall, Ruth Painter. *Mary Lincoln, Biography of a Marriage*. Boston: Little, Brown and Co., 1953

Report of the Joint Committee on the Conduct of the War, 38th Congress, 2nd Session, 1865, Report No. 142.

Sheridan, Philip, *Personal Memoirs*, 2 vols. 1888.

*Sherman's Selected Correspondence of the Civil War*, Brooks D. Simpson and Jean V. Berlin, ed., Chapel Hill: The University of North Carolina Press, 1999.

Sherman, John. *John Sherman's Recollections of Forty Years in the House, Senate and Cabinet: An Autobiography*. Chicago: Werner Co., 1895.

Sherman, William Tecumseh. *Memoirs of General W. T. Sherman*. New York: Literary Classics of the United States, 1990. Originally published New York: D. Appleton and Co., 2 vols., 1875.

Simon, John Y. ed. *The Personal Memoirs of Julia Dent Grant*. New York: Putnam, 1975.

Simon, John Y., ed. *The Papers of Ulysses S. Grant*. 18 vols. Carbondale: Southern Illinois University Press 1967-1991.

Stern, Philip Van Doren. *An End to Valor*. Boston: The Riverside Press Cambridge, 1958.

Steward, N. B. *Dan McCook's Regiment, 52nd O.V.I. ... .*, 1900.

Symonds, Craig L. *Joseph E. Johnston, A Civil War Biography*. New York: W.W. Norton & Co., 1992.

*The Selected Papers of Thaddeus Stevens*, 2 vols, Beverly Wilson Palmer and Holly Byers Ochoa, ed., University of Pittsburgh Press, 1998.

Turner, Justin G. and Turner, Linda Levitt. *Mary Todd Lincoln, Her Life and Letters*. New York: Alfred A. Knopf, 1972.

Vetter, Charles E. *Sherman: Merchant of Terror, Advocate of Peace*. Louisiana: Pelican Publishing Co. Inc., 1992.

*War of the Rebellion ... Official Records of the Union and Confederate Armies*, 128 vols., 1880-1901.

Welles, Gideon. *Diary of Gideon Welles, Secretary of the Navy under Lincoln and Johnson*. 3 vols., Boston: Houghton Mifflin Co., 1911.

Woodward, C. Vann, ed., *Mary Chestnut's Civil War*. New Haven: Yale University Press, 1981.

## Newspapers

*Baltimore Sun*
*Chicago Evening Journal*
*Chicago Tribune*
*Cincinnati Commercial*
*Daily Illinois State Journal*
*Frank Leslie's Illustrated Newspaper*
*Harper's Weekly*
*New York Herald*
*New York Times*
*New York Tribune*
*New York World*
*Philadelphia Evening Bulletin*
*Philadelphia Inquirer*
*Sacramento Daily Union*
*The National Tribune*
*Washington Daily Morning Chronicle*
*Washington Evening Star*

## Abbreviations

| SSCCW | Sherman's Selected Correspondence of the Civil War |
|---|---|
| SM | Sherman's Memoirs |
| GM | Grant's Memoirs |
| OR | War of the Rebellion ... Official Records of the Union and Confederate Armies |

## Notes

### Profiles

Alfriend, *Historical Times Illustrated,* Marszalek, Flower, Hyman, Baker, Catton, Grant.

### Prologue
### Politics of War

1.  *Historical Times Illustrated.*
2.  Marszalek, page 311.
3.  OR, I, 44, pages 797-98.
4.  Marszalek, page 212.
5.  Marszalek, page 114.
6.  OR, I, 47, pt. 2, pages 543-44; a letter to Kilpatrick.
7.  Marszalek, page 251.
8.  Lincoln Papers, 1864, pages 181-2
9.  L. Lewis, pages 410- 12.
10. OR, I, 47, pt. 2, pages 4-5, letter to Halleck.
11. L. Lewis, page 411.
12. L. Lewis, page 394.
13. L. Lewis, page 393.
14. Fellman, page 162; L. Lewis, page 392; Glatthaar, page 67.
15. Fellman, page 162.
16. Flower, pages 182-84.
17. Brewer, war success, page 165; jobs by blacks, page 13; owners fined, page 9. Jefferson Davis, *The Almanac of American History*, page 293.
18. Flower, page 189.
19. Welles, vol. I, page 58.
20. Flower, page 116.
21. Hyman, pages 131-35.
22. Hyman, page 233.
23. McPherson, *Ordeal by Fire*, pages 350-51; Flower, page 186; Donald, Lincoln wanted to vote bill, pages 364-65.
24. Flower, page 232.
25. Carpenter, page 306.
26. Carpenter, page 306.
27. Flower, page 188.
28. L. Lewis, pages 391 and 394.
29. Grant Papers, vol. 15, page 238.
30. Fellman, page 164; "Mad Incorruptible," L. Lewis, *Myths of Lincoln*, page 50.
31. Flower, page 78.
32. Flower, page 253.

33. Bates, page 392.
34. GM, page 580.
35. Flower, page 216.
36. Flower, page 217.
37. Flower, page 127.
38. Flower, pages 126-27.
39. Bates, page 400.
40. Flower, pages 369-70.
41. OR, I, 47, pt 2, pages 4-5.
42. Fellman, page 163; Salmon P. Chase's letter to Sherman, January 2, 1865.
43. The *New York Herald,* December 28, 1864, page 8.
44. OR, I, 47, pt 2, pages 36-37.
45. SM, pages 722, 730, 725.
46. Fellman, page 164; SM, page 729.
47. Flower, page 188, see also Ezell, page 50.
48. Dana, page 192.
49. Dana, "The Great Energy," page 157; Dana, page 289.
50. Welles, Stanton's navy, vol. 1, page 67.
51. Connolly, page 373.
52. Fitch, page 236.
53. Connolly, pages 354 and 373.
54. OR, I, 47, pt. 2, page 36; Davis' report, OR, I, 44, pages 166-68.
55. OR, I, 47, pt 2, pages 37-41.
56. SM, page 727.
57. Flower, Saxton's title, page 186; Flower, Stanton's quote, page 298.
58. Special Orders No. 15, OR, I, 47, pt 2, pages 60-62; Thaddeus Stevens, L. Lewis, page 480.
59. Flower, page 298.
60. Grant Papers, page 272.
61. Howe, pages 327-28.
62. SM, page 729.
63. McPherson, *The Negro's Civil War*, page 304.
64. Welles, vol. II, page 228; "pay court," vol. II, page 297.

**Forage Liberally**
**Bummers Invade the South**

1. Hyman, page 345.
2. Glatthaar, pages 19 and 54.
3. Jones, page 281.
4. Glatthaar, page 120.
5. Hedley, page 269; Glatthaar, page 123.
6. Hedley, page 269.
7. Jones, pages 49-59.
8. Jones, page 39.
9. Glatthaar, page 123.
10. Jones, page 59.
11. Hedley, page 269.
12. Glatthaar, page 126.
13. Glatthaar, page 124.
14. Jones, page 78.
15. Jones, page 81.
16. Glatthaar, page 128; OR, I, 47, pt. 2, pages 545-44.

17. Hyman, page 342.
18. SM, page 810.
19. *Cincinnati Commercial*, December 12, 1864, page 3.
20. Glatthaar, page 69.
21. L. Lewis, pages 395 and 512.
22. L. Lewis, Lincoln re-elected, page 394; Brooks, national thanks, page 172.
23. *Cincinnati Commercial,* December 27, 1864, page 2.
24. OR, I, 44, pages 798-800.
25. Vetter, page 249.
26. L. Lloyd, page 511.
27. L. Lewis, page 504.
28. L. Lewis, page 506.
29. Marszalek, pages 324-25.
30. GM, pages 541-42.
31. Carpenter, page 266.

### Second Inaugural
### With Malice Toward None

1. Stern, page 8.
2. Welles, vol. 2, page 252.
3. Brooks, page 211.
4. Stern, page 12.
5. Baker, page 250.

### Lee Surrenders to Grant
### Stanton Offers His Resignation

1. OR, I, 44, pages 138-140.
2. OR, I, 44, page 140.
3. Glatthaar, page 179.
4. OR, I, 47, pt. 3, page 177.
5. Carpenter, page 265.

### Sherman and Johnston
### 'We Shall Have News Soon'

1. Carpenter, page 292; Welles, vol. 2, pages 280-83.
2. OR, I, 47, pt. 3, page 207.
3. OR, I, 47, pt. 3, page 221.
4. SM, page 836.
5. L. Lewis, 534-35; SM, pages 836-37.
6. Symonds, page 355 and SM, page 837.
7. Johnston, page 402; SM, page 837.
8. Symonds, page 326.
9. Crozier, page 397.
10. Symonds, page 331.
11. Symonds, page 329
12. Symonds, page 329.
13. Symonds, page 354.
14. Alfriend, Davis' and Johnston's quotes, pages 623-26.
15. Symonds, pages 354-55.

16. Johnston, pages 402- 03.
17. L. Lewis, page 535.
18. Johnston, page 404.
19. SM, page 840.
20. Symonds, page 356.
21. SM, page 838.
22. L. Lewis, page 539.
23. SM, page 841.
24. Johnston, pages 403-05.
25. Symonds, page 356.
26. OR, I, 47, pt. 3, pages 243-45; SM, page 841.
27. Stern, page 328.
28. Howe, page 344.
29. OR, I, 47, pt. 3, page 245.

## Terms Denied
## Has Sherman Gone Mad?

1. Marszalek, page 346.
2. Bates, page 396.
3. Welles, vol. 2, page 295.
4. Welles, page 295.
5. Bates, page 424.
6. OR, I, 47, pt. 3, page 302.
7. *New York Times* April, 23, 1865.
8. Welles pages 296-97.
9. OR, I, 47, pt. 3, page 277.
10. Marszalek, page 347.
11. SM, page 219.
12. L. Lewis, page 193.
13. SM, pages 219-20 and L. Lewis, page 194.
14. Marszalek, page 162.
15. SM, page 221.
16. Marszalek, page 164.
17. OR, I, 52, pt. 1, page 198.
18. Marszalek, page 174.
19. John Sherman, page 214.
20. SSCCW, page 174.
21. SM, page 846.
22. SM, page 852.
23. Grant Papers, Vol. 15, page 13.
24. L. Lewis, page 557. Gen. Carl Schurz was a general on Sherman's staff.
25. Hatcher, page 330.
26. OR, I, 47, pt. 3, page 302.
27. Grant Papers, page 15.
28. OR, II, 47, pt. 3, pages 334-35.
29. L. Lewis, page 558.
30. Howe, page 350
31. Flower, page 265; McAllister, page 303.
32. Lewis, page 559; Grant to Halleck, OR, I, 47, pt. 3, page, 313
33. OR, I, 47, pt. 3. pages 411-12.

34.  OR, I, 47, pt. 3, pages 411-12.
35.  SM, page 862.
36.  SSCCW, page 891.
37.  OR, I, 47, pt. 3, pages 411-12.
38.  OR, I, 47, pt. 3, page 406.
39.  Howe, page 351.
40.  SM, pages 861-62.

**Return to Richmond**
**The Nerve of Halleck**

1.   Glatthaar, page 179.
2.   Glatthaar, page 179.
3.   Glatthaar, page 179.
4.   OR, I, 47, pt. 3, page 434.
5.   OR, I, 38: pt. 5, pages 791-94.
6.   OR, I, 47, pt. 3, pages 454-55.
7.   Lewis, page 564.
8.   Lewis, page 565.
9.   Howe, page 353.
10.  SM, page 863.
11.  OR, I, 47, pt. 3, page 433, Sherman to Grant.
12.  OR, I, 47, pt. 3, page 441; Grant quote, OR, I, 47, pt. 3, page 445.
13.  OR, I, 47, pt. 3, page 435.
14.  OR, I, 47, pt. 3, page 454.
15.  OR, I, 47, pt. 3, page 454.
16.  OR, I, 47, pt. 3, page 455.
17.  Howe, page 353.
18.  L. Lewis, page 560.
19.  Grant Papers, vol. 15, page 74.
20.  Howe, page 353.
21.  Marszalek, page 353; Bruke Davis, page 282.
22.  OR, II, 47, pt. 3, pages 477-78.
23.  Howe, page 353.

**Time to Go Home**
**The Eve of the Grand Review**

1.   Glatthaar, page 179.
2.   SM, page 864.
3.   Grant Papers, vol. 15, page 73.
4.   OR,  I, 47, pt. 3, page 531.
5.   Grant Papers, vol. 15, page 73.
6.   Catton, Halleck as Grant's friend, page 15; GM, page 167.
7.   GM, page 167.
8.   Catton, page 15.
9.   GM, page 168.
10.  GM, page 168.
11.  GM, page 168.
12.  GM, page 196.
13.  GM, page 197.
14.  GM, page 200.
15.  Howe, page 278.

16. SM, page 864.
17. SM, page 864.
18. Grant Papers, vol. 15, page 74.
19. Newspapers April 19, 1865.
20. Flower, page 288.
21. Flower, page 368.
22. Flower, page 288.
23. *New York Times*, May 24, 1865.
24. Newspaper accounts.
25. Stern, page 343 and newspaper accounts. John M. Forbes, *New York Tribune*, May 23, 1865.
26. Grant Papers, page 478.
27. L. Lewis, page 567 and *New York Tribune*, May, 22, 1865, page 8.
28. Report of the Committee on the Conduct of War, 38th Congress, 2nd session (Washington, D.C., 1865), vol. 3.
29. Ibid.
30. Howe, page 353.
31. L. Lewis, page 567
32. Newspaper accounts, May 22, 1865.
33. *Chicago Evening Post*, February 11, 1893 and Horan, page 63.
34. Horan, page 63.
35. Marszalek, page 354.
36. Merrill, page 299.
37. Fellman, page 252, and Mahon, page 26.
38. OR, 47: pt. 3, page 576.
39. Halsey, page 207.
40. Glatthaar, page 180.
41. Halsey, page 208.
42. Glatthaar, page 181.
43. Halsey, page 209.
44. James Nichol, unpublished letter dated May 23, 1865. Manuscript group 10273, the York County Heritage Trust.
45. Chamberlain, pages 320-25.

## The President's Been Shot
## Farewell, Mary Todd Lincoln

1. Donald, page 597.
2. Flower, page 281.
3. Flower, page 282.
4. Donald, page 598.
5. Flower, page 282.
6. Baker, page 250.
7. Dana, page 277.
8. Dana, page 278.
9. Flower, page 282.
10. Flower, page 283.
11. Donald, pages 598-99; Flower, page 283.
12. Baker, page 247.
13. Keckley, page 191.
14. Baker, page 250; Keckley, pages 199-200.

The date that Mary Todd Lincoln left the White House for the final time remains debatable. Why is this fact important? Because modern history can tell us confidently the dates that Eleanor Roosevelt and Jacqueline Kennedy vacated the White House after the deaths of their husbands. But the departure of Mrs. Lincoln has not been pinned down.

Mary Todd Lincoln, the first wife of a U.S. president to be assassinated, left Washington heart-broken and grieving during one of the proudest moments in the nation's history, the Grand Review.

So when did she leave? These are the facts.

Mrs. Lincoln left during the evening hours of either Monday, May 22, or Tuesday, May 23, 1865, and boarded a 6 p.m. train for Chicago.

Some historians have written that she left on the first day of the Grand Review, May 23. Other historians believe she left May 22, the day before the event.

Enter a never-published letter Mrs. Lincoln wrote to a Madame Berghmans that sold at Christie's Auction in New York in December 1999. Mrs. Lincoln wrote: "We leave here, tomorrow evening, yet I do not feel as if I could do so, without bidding you farewell. I go hence, a broken-hearted woman, without my beloved Husband, who was everything to me. I do not have the least desire to live." Mrs. Lincoln asks Madame Berghmans to visit her "tomorrow about three o'clock." She ends the letter with "God alone knows the agony of this crushed heart." (Christie's Auction, New York City, December 1999, Lot 142.)

The letter is dated May 22, 1865. Based on this letter, Mrs. Lincoln would have left the White House on May 23. But, as any Mary Todd Lincoln historian will point out, she was prone to write the wrong dates on her letters, as were many other people of that time.

The primary sources in this question are newspapers. Nearly all newspapers carried a short story about Mrs. Lincoln leaving the White House with her two sons and others. This is where the problem lies.

The majority of newspapers that carried this story reported it in their May 23, 1865, editions. But nearly all theses stories had a dateline of May 22 above the story, meaning the news was learned on that day.

The *Washington Evening Star* reported in its May 22, 1865, evening edition: "Mrs. Lincoln has decided upon leaving Washington this afternoon at 6 o'clock for her home in Springfield, Ill. She will be accompanied by Capt. Robert Lincoln, Master Tad Lincoln and others."

The *New York Times* reported on May 18, 1865, that "Mrs. Lincoln will vacate the President's mansion on Monday next (May 22)."

Another issue involves Mrs. Lincoln's sons. Robert Lincoln was a captain in the army and a member of Grant's "military family." Actually, President Lincoln had asked Grant to provide a position for his Harvard-educated son "who wishes to see something of the war before it ends." Lincoln told Grant that he did not want Robert placed into the ranks and said he and not the public would take care of Robert's pay. (*The Collected Works of Abraham Lincoln*, vol. 8, pages 223-24.)

When newspapers reported that Grant and his staff had arrived on the first day of the Grand Review, Robert Lincoln's name was not mentioned. Plus, Robert Lincoln's biographer never connects him to the Grand Review.

Mrs. Lincoln's other son, Tad, was an energetic young man who some say was a slow learner. In a playful act, Secretary of War Stanton dubbed Tad a lieutenant in the army. The boy took his new title seriously and one day relieved the White House sentries from duty, leaving the building unguarded for a night. (Baker, page 255, slow learner; Brooks, page 252, Tad and Stanton.)

Tad also enjoyed watching soldiers in parades, and various soldiers, while saluting government and military officials, sometimes would add the call "three cheers for the boy." (Brooks, page 251.)

He certainly would have been drawn to the White House gate to watch the Grand Review.

If Tad Lincoln were in Washington during the Grand Review, Elizabeth Keckley, Mrs. Lincoln's friend, confidant and personal seamstress, never mentions it in her book. Keckley writes only about how hardly anyone had come to say goodbye when Mrs. Lincoln left.

Mrs. Lincoln likely would not have stayed for the Grand Review when her "beloved Husband" was not present, and the "wicked" new president, Andrew Johnson, the man who made the drunken speech at the second inaugural, the man who she believed conspired to kill her husband, was sitting in the center of the grandstand. (Baker, page 250.)

But the most telling of all the suppositions is that none of the hundreds of letters Mrs. Lincoln wrote contains a comment on the May 23 and 24 festivities.

According to railroad records, the train ride from Washington to Chicago was about 842 miles. The train carrying Mrs. Lincoln, who with her party traveled in a private car, first stopped in Baltimore, Maryland. The train also made stops in Pennsylvania in cities such as York, Harrisburg, Altoona and Pittsburgh, as well as in Rochester. In Ohio, it stopped in Alliance, Mansfield and Lima, and in Indiana, in Fort Wayne, Plymouth and Valparaiso. The average speed of the train was about 20 mph. The trip took nearly 42 hours and would have landed Mrs. Lincoln in Chicago at 12:30 p.m. Chicago time. (*Appletons' Railway and Steam Navigation Guide*, D. Appleton & Co., Broadway, New York, 1865. Pages 118 through 252.)

Newspapers in Illinois announced Mrs. Lincoln's arrival in Chicago. The *Illinois State Journal* and the *Chicago Evening Journal* reported that Mrs. Lincoln arrived Wednesday afternoon, May 24, and stayed at the Tremont House.

Based on the information from the primary sources, railroad records and Mrs. Lincoln herself, we must conclude that the wife of President Lincoln left the White House on May 22, 1865 — the day before the Grand Review.

15. Keckley, page 208.

### Day One of the Grand Review
### 'Get Out of the Way, You Fool!'

1.   Chamberlain, page, 329. May 24, 1865, newspaper accounts.
2.   Hatcher, page 354.
3.   Brooks, Page 273.
4.   May 24, 1865, newspaper accounts.
5.   May 24, 1865, newspaper accounts.
6.   May 24, 1865, newspaper accounts.
7.   May 24, 1865, newspaper accounts.
8.   May 24, 1865, newspaper accounts.
9.   *Chicago Tribune*, May, 24, 1865.
10.  Cleaves, page 339 and Crozier, 419.
11.  Cleaves, page 124.
12.  Donald, page 447.
13.  Crozier, page 419.
14.  *New York World*, May, 24, 1865, page 1.
15.  *New York Tribune*, May, 24, 1865.
16.  GM, page 581.
17.  Grant Papers, vol. 15, page 44 and Sheridan Memoirs, page 210.
18.  Sheridan Memoirs, page 209.
19.  *New York Herald*, May 24, 1865, page 1.
20.  Flower, page 288.
21.  Flower, page 288.
22.  Hedley, page 462.
23.  *New York Tribune*, page 1.
24.  May 24, 1865 newspapers accounts.
25.  *The National Tribune*, August 12, 1915, Fairfax, Custer's horse's name, page 58.
26.  *The National Tribune*, August 12, 1915.
27.  Brooks, page 275.
28.  "Custer Tie" and Zouaves, May 24, 1865, newspapers.
29.  Brooks, page 275.

30. Porter, pages 508-09.
31. Brooks, page 275.
32. Sanitary Commission, *New York Tribune*, May, 25, 1865; Porter, flag, page 508.
33. Fitch, page 344.
34. Halsey, page 210.
35. Halsey, page 210.
36. OR, 47: pt. 3, page 443 and *New York World*, May 25, 1865.
37. *Chicago Tribune*, story dated May 23, 1865.
38. L. Lewis, pages 572-73.
39. Marszalek, page 355.
40. Porter, Johnson's hat, page 508; crowd cheers, May 24, 1865, newspapers.
41. Chamberlain, page 342.
42. Brooks, page 276.
43. *Washington Daily Chronicle* May 24.
44. Brooks, page 279.
45. Brooks, page 277.
46. The *Washington Daily Chronicle*, May 24, 1865.
47. May 24, 1865, newspapers.
48. The *Washington Daily Chronicle*, *Washington Evening Star* and *New York Tribune*.
49. Chamberlain, pages 372-73.
50. Grant Papers, vol. 15, pages 98-99.
51. The *New York Tribune*, May 23, 1865, page 4.
52. The *Cincinnati Commercial*, May 25, 1865.

## Day Two of the Grand Review
## The Look of a Proud Conqueror

1. The *Baltimore Sun*, May, 24, 1865, page 8.
2. The *Cincinnati Commercial*, May 25, 1865.
3. L. Lewis, page 573.
4. The *Cincinnati Commercial*, May, 24, 1865.
5. The *Chicago Tribune*, May, 25, 1865.
6. The *New York Herald*, May 24, 1865, page 1.
7. The *New York Herald*, May, 24, 1865, page 1.
8. The *Baltimore Sun*, May, 25, 1865, page 8.
9. *National Tribune*, March 26, 1896.
10. Brooks, church clocks, page 279; signal gun, *Cincinnati Commercial*, May 25, 1865; SM, Atlanta in 1864, page 656; Howard riding with Sherman, *National Tribune*, March 26, 1896.
11. Brooks, page 279.
12. The *Chicago Tribune*, May, 24, 1865.
13. Women on balconies, *Cincinnati Commercial*, May 25, 1865, page 2; L. Lewis, "hold eyes front," page 574.
14. Fairfax, page 73.
15. L. Lewis, page 573.
16. SM, page 866; and newspapers.
17. *Cincinnati Commercial*, May 24, 1865; and L. Lewis, page 516.
18. SM, page 865.
19. The *New York Times*, May, 25, 1865.
20. Holloway, O.O. Howard, page 132; Brooks, Sherman, page 278.
21. Brooks, page 278.
22. Brooks, page 279.
23. Newspapers.

24. Brooks, dark scar, page 279; L. Lewis, page 577.
25. Dana, page 290.
26. SM, page 866.
27. Flower, page 288.
28. Flower, page 288.
29. Hatcher, pages 382-83.
30. Hatcher, page 401.
31. Halsey, page 211.
32. GM, page 579.
33. L. Lewis, pages 575-76.
34. Halsey, page 211.
35. Glatthaar, page 181.
36. Newspapers.
37. Lewis, page 576.
38. Porter, pages 509-11.
39. Newspapers, May 25, 1865.
40. Newspapers, May 25, 1865.
41. Marszalek, page 357.

## Museum Section

Profile and artifact descriptions, *Historical Times Illustrated Encyclopedia of the Civil War.*

# Index